TABLE OF CONTENTS

DO YOU WANNA DANCE?

My youthful days are far behind me, disappearing rapidly in the rear-view mirror of life. Now that I have crossed the Rubicon of retirement from the working world—and as a retired high school teacher, I no longer must respond to children's demands, parental false expectations, nor a principal's list of "dos" or "don'ts" at staff meetings—I have signalled a move to the slow lane, a lane I have been following for several years, unless, of course, our dental hygienist decides that my teeth and my wife's teeth must be inspected and cleaned at 8:30 a.m. Thus, to appease the dentist, who apparently shows a great deal of concern for the remaining teeth in our heads, my wife and I found ourselves caught at 8:10 a.m., in the ritual most of the working world participates in, not once but twice daily, a ritual called, for some bizarre reason, "rush hour."

My thoughts, as our car crawled along in stop-and-go segments on that now rare 8:10 a.m. drive, returned to those days in Churchill in the 1950s, where a four-car lineup at a stop sign would bring the locals out to stare in wonder at the rare phenomenon. It was treated with the same awe and reverence as a full solar eclipse.

Slowly moving north, over a bridge that spans the Assiniboine River, I thought back to my early days in that remote northern town. Rivers always remind me of Churchill, a place that is perched on the very cusp of the Churchill River estuary, a river that is one of Canada's great and historic waterways. My thoughts took me back to a cool, rainy summer morning in July, where a woman and two boys in tow were hesitant to leave the comfort of a CN sleeper car. On the platform waited a man, there to greet the woman and the two boys. I was one of those boys, the older and certainly the more handsome of the two. The woman was my Mother, who, upon seeing the man, my Father, flew into his waiting arms, while my brother and I blinked and stared into the apparently empty colour-washed world we had inherited. But I was wrong. Although I didn't then know it, I was about to take a decade-long ride that would colour my perception of the world and build a firm and solid belief system that would guide me through life.

As I have broadly hinted, I am a senior citizen, and the kids I hung with are cruising down the same highway, if they have not already reluctantly motored off down an exit ramp onto Sunset Street, like so many of the pop stars we listened to on the radio or scratchy 45s. And despite the decades, it all still feels like yesterday. The kids I ran with are still fifteen. The boys are scruffy in their blue jeans, Hush Puppies, T-shirts, and well-worn, passed-down parkas or spring jackets, and they still smell of greasy hair product, which we smoothed on our hair to create fabulous "ducktails" or to glue the hair down to the side of our heads. The girls, still cute as ever, favour ponytails, fluffy pink, or blue sweaters, and I am happy to say, "short shorts," which always seem to be white. I also recall the ache of muscles we rarely exercised until we had a summer job and a hot date—not with a girl in white short shorts, but instead, a date with a shovel, a pile of gravel, and a concrete mixer—or the ache of the heart when your girl left town with her family for a new military posting far, far away.

The Churchill years were few, but those years were at a critical time in the making of me—although, at the time, I did not know it. The North, the isolation, the close-knit fabric of a small community at the end of the line gave me and my friends a freedom to do things other kids our age living elsewhere could only dream of. Where else on earth could one be guaranteed a chance meeting with a great white bear, which was hopefully not hungry; experience the wonders of the Northern Lights as they dance in an infinite wave of colours and patterns across the sky's ballroom; watch rockets hurl themselves at mind-bending speeds into the depths of space; smell the bush on a hot summer day, a pungent earthy aroma that, in quiet moments, I reinvent in my mind; relish the clean, cold taste of water straight from a river or stream; walk for miles in the bush, hearing only the sound of your footsteps or the rustle of the trees, the near silence only punctuated by the sudden, urgent cry of a bird; or breathe in the clean, fresh sea air as we walk the rocks and beach of the Bay on a fine June evening?

These are the years, coloured and rounded, of course, by the passage of time, the hard edges softened but still there—memories whirling and twirling, memories of people and places and things found in a different time.

Welcome to my memories. Welcome to the 1950s. Welcome to Churchill. My hometown.

THE PERNICIOUS POOL
HALL SAGA, 1959

Arctic Alleys, the local pool hall and bowling alley, loomed large in my fifteen-year-old universe, a time when a confusing series of hormone-driven changes within me caused the ground to shift beneath my feet, a time when the horror of an adolescent facial zit swelled to the size of Europe. Yes, the pool hall offered shiny balls and coloured lights, attractions for one who had yet to learn that shiny balls and coloured lights were just distractions from reality.

The pool hall, with its noisy, carnival-like atmosphere, was a convenient short stroll from the after-school bus parked next to the flagpole and the two cannons in the town square. And predictably, as at most carnivals, there were also the same kind of inhabitants there. Always there. Shifty types who apparently rarely worked, did not go to school, and did nothing constructive that anyone would say contributed in a positive way to society. They gathered in groups of two or three—dark, scary, shadowy spectres, smoking copious cigarettes—and neither I nor my friends would dare to bother them, for fear they might beat us up. We were, after all, fifteen-year-olds, and most of the permanent pool hall inhabitants appeared to be much older, perhaps seventeen.

The fact that we attended school, and they didn't, created a huge gulf between us. We had little in common. And if we were fortunate to find a vacant table, they leaned against the wall and made somewhat degrading comments about our manhood, our lineage, or our skills, and occasionally pushed the end of a cue when someone was about to make a clincher of a shot. Oh, how we hated them and talked bravely amongst ourselves of

John Horner

"giving it" to one or more of our tormentors. Fortunately, Jim, the proprietor of the pool hall and alleys, and his daughter, kept things peaceful. Lord knows what we might have done to those pool hall carnival dwellers had they not continually kept an eye on things.

Insofar as being able to play pool, I must reluctantly count myself in the realm of those who had little skill, and an ability not to improve, no matter how many games I played. Maybe it was because I refused to wear my glasses, generously provided to me by the old man. But more about those later.

My Father disapproved of a few things. Actually, not true! He disapproved of lots of things. And he really disapproved of the pool hall and my going there. Not that he disapproved of billiards. He was good at the game. No! He disapproved of the element who hung out there, in the pool hall. He made it clear I was not to go there. I was directed to go straight home, even if my friends did not. "Would you jump off a cliff if they did?" he asked. It was obviously a rhetorical question, as he always added, "Of course not." However, as I got off the bus at half past four, and Dad got home around half past five, or even quarter to six, that allowed me a good hour to pursue my growing lack of skill playing the game.

Now about those glasses. On my fifteenth birthday, I was prescribed glasses by a visiting optometrist who came to Churchill twice a year, as I had difficulty seeing things, even the blackboard at school. The glasses were ordered, and shortly thereafter, they arrived from Winnipeg at our post office box. Upon putting them on, I was amazed at how clear, how sharply defined, and how beautiful the world was, especially girls.

But they were still glasses, ugly and uncool. Thus, in the morning, I would leave home with glasses on, watched by a smiling Mother. Upon turning the corner, I would whip them off and put them in my parka pocket. My world then reverted to the customary blurry way I had seen it for years. After all, geeks wore glasses, and the consequent teasing, if worn, would not have been worth the benefits of wearing them.

The glasses would then reside in my parka pocket, in my locker, in school, for the entire day, and only reappear upon my returning home in the evening. Then, the horror of the predictable happened. I was playing pool with my usual skill, and the sneers of the unemployed layabouts who held up the walls, and attempted a difficult shot, which meant half climbing and

6

lying on the table, a feat that today I recognize only the young can do. As I clutched the cue, I heard a sound and felt something snap and give in my parka pocket. Terrified, I slid off the table, put my hand inside the pocket, and felt, in two neat pieces, my new glasses, purchased by my dad so that I could see clearly. I was a dead man. What could I say to him? The truth? "I was playing pool, Dad, in the pool hall where you told me not to go, without my glasses on, and they broke in my pocket playing pool." Now that would be suicidal or homicidal, depending upon who did what to whom.

It was Wayne, who also occasionally wore dark horn-rimmed glasses, who offered the most plausible explanation, hopefully from past experience. "You put 'em in your pocket for protection." From what, he didn't say. "And you got off the bus, slipped on some ice, fell on your side, and they broke," he finished, with a flourish of his hand, like a magician after a trick.

Simple to say, but the real magic was to lie to the old man and fool him and not look guilty. The result was a convoluted story that grew with each lie. "There were lots of people around me pushing as I got off the bus . . . and I fell . . . and they fell on me . . . and my glasses got broken . . . and I'm so sorry Dad." And I'm sure he didn't believe a word I said, but I never once mentioned the pool hall, and thankfully, he never brought it up. Why should he? And a month later, new replacement glasses arrived from Winnipeg in our post office box. I still never wore them, but this time, I kept them safe in the case provided.

Once in a while, the bowling alleys, another part of Jim's pool hall empire, offered the gullible the chance of earning spare cash by setting pins as a pin boy. There were four lanes, and they were often busy with bowlers bouncing balls down the well-worn, battle-scarred lanes. And these lanes, unlike those found in modern, slick, glow-ball bowling alleys, were not automated. You see, these lanes, unlike today's alleys equipped with robotic pin setters, needed someone dumb enough to be at the pin end of the alley to manually set the pins after they were literally bowled over. And sometimes, that "someone dumb enough" was me. My old man would not have been amused had he known I occasionally waited at the receiving end of a cannonball-sized, rock-hard ball, cast at great speed and doubtful accuracy toward the still-standing pins and me. It was akin to being at the wrong end of a firing range, with people taking pot shots at me. And, to make things even more interesting, each pin boy had two lanes to look after. Today, I would pass from this mortal coil, having had a cardiac arrest within minutes, leaping like a banshee from one lane to the next. And, as an extra treat, the pin boy also had to recover the balls and return them down the rail to the bowlers. On more than one occasion, a bowler would ignore etiquette and, while I was in the process of retrieving a ball, hurl a ball down the lane. I prefer to believe that this was an oversight on the part of the bowler and not a serious attempt to kill or maim me. Fortunately, for me, I survived intact. And for this, I was paid two bits per lane per game and a free fountain cola. Usually, the bowlers added a two-bit tip. One dollar for around forty-five minutes. Not a lot. But enough to meet my basic needs.

And then there was Karen who was the youngest daughter of a local businessman and, like me, made her way to the alleys after school. She flirted with the pool hall inhabitants, who spent the winter months hibernating there. Karen was fifteen, cute, and I had a distant crush on her. I say "distant" because I believed she was unobtainable. So, I worshipped her from afar. I'm sure she knew. No! I know she knew, and she played me like a piano. Occasionally, on the crowded bus ride home from school, she would sit on my knee with one arm carelessly resting around my neck. For me, this was both agony and ecstasy. She was, in my estimation, beautiful, and I was smitten. She was my age, perhaps slightly younger, but she was in most ways older than me. I am sure you know what I mean. Some boys simply take longer to grow up. Boys are gawky and awkward, whereas girls of a similar age are not and have the gift of attracting mature, worldly seventeen-year-old males by batting their eyelashes and sharing a cigarette in the back of the pool hall. Yes, I hated those guys. Really, really hated them.

A big attraction of the alleys was the jukebox, a machine that blared the music belonging to that particular time. The jukebox was filled with the latest selection of 45s: one play for a nickel, two plays for a dime, and five plays for a quarter. There, I was introduced to Bobby Darren's "Dream Lover," Tommy Roe's "Sheila," the Everlys' "Cathy's Clown," all very nice people, I'm sure, and all swimming in Phil Phillips's "Sea of Love," only to be washed away by the Cascades' "Rhythm of the Rain." Unfortunately, there was also a selection of country songs, songs that mostly complained bitterly about how "My baby's gone to town in my pickup with my best friend," songs favoured by the pool hall inhabitants, songs that I studiously ignored. I hated country music just as much as I hated those older guys who surrounded Karen, who was still there, smoking and batting her eyelashes at them in the back of the pool hall. I was, I knew, "Born Too Late."

But that was long ago. Today, as I sit and ruminate over the past, it is beyond a doubt that the music of that era has the power to take me back to a hazy, smoke-filled pool hall, a time when despite the frightening reality of the Cold War, Sonny James sang optimistically of "Young Love." Music is the link to a time and place I once inhabited. A certain song transports the mind to those golden times. They were probably not so golden, but memory is oh so selective.

So, there you have it. Arctic Alleys. The pool hall and the bowling alleys. Susie and the jukebox. The chain-smoking ne'er-do-wells. The alleys, right behind my house. And now, in the autumn of life, I am stretched to explain why such a place was the attraction it was. Perhaps my Dad was right. It was no place for a kid to hang out. But kids being kids, who listens to their dads anyway?

LET'S TWIST AGAIN

The two decades that straddled the mid-twentieth century saw a seismic shift in postwar global power and culture with the emergence of the Soviet Union in the east and, in the west, the United States—combatants in a new kind of deep and silent war we call the "Cold War." American troops were stationed on bases worldwide to counter this threat, a threat, we were told, intent on destroying us. We, in Churchill, were but a tiny part of this equation, this expensive, insane, possibly catastrophic military standoff. The reverse of the same coin was the dominance of American culture, a culture spread by Hollywood movies and the television we watched, the music we listened to, and the books and magazines we read. And like most teenagers, we eagerly followed the siren call of slick American pop culture. It was inescapable. Then, to throw the United States into a tizzy of self-doubt and a realization that buckets of money were to be spent immediately on science, was the Soviets' launch of Sputnik, a shiny basketball-sized satellite. We listened and wondered in awe at the sound of this silver ball as it beeped its way in slowly decreasing orbits around earth, causing, in the autumn of 1957, much celebration and jubilation in Moscow and, in Washington, a rising fear of being left behind, cutting deeply into the wounded American psyche and swagger. Kennedy's response, at his 1961 inauguration, was the outrageous promise to "have a man on the moon by the end of this decade." In August of 1969, this promise was kept, a remarkable achievement.

By the early '60s, we were also to be mesmerized by the horrors of the war raging in far-off Vietnam, as graphic images from the jungle killing floor flickered across local cinema screens on the Movie tone or Pathé Newsreels or shared time and space with the evening pork chops or fried chicken supper, the evening television news brought to you by your favourite brand of detergent or coffee.

Those mid-century decades were the age of rocket-inspired car design, complete with sharp-edged fins and large, circular taillights that mimicked a missile in flight, cars that would deliver the new-moneyed middle class to their cookie-cutter new homes built on the periphery of cities, built in areas created by car ownership, the cow pastures turned into real estate we called "suburbia." And those mid-twentieth century cars were built with style but never substance. Even an accident at a moderate speed in one of those cars, when returning home to one of those cookie-cutter homes built in a bland "looks the same" neighbourhood, was almost guaranteed to kill or maim the driver or passengers. Safe cars and seatbelts were not then a concern to the manufacturer. Style was.

This was a time when laboratories and researchers concocted a witch's brew of new products. Thalidomide, which certainly alleviated the effects of morning sickness in women during the early stages of pregnancy, left in its wake a stream of limbless babies as a side effect. Agent Orange, a delightful-sounding product, was designed to defoliate the jungles of Vietnam and Cambodia, leaving in its slipstream leukemia, Hodgkin's disease, and a platter full of cancers. Napalm was used to incinerate those left hiding in the leafless jungles and, as another side effect, burned alive women and children caught in the crossfire. And then there was the birth control pill, generically and simply referred to as "the pill." Domestically, the pill was most controversial and revolutionary—controversial especially by those who saw the decline and fall of civilisation and morality in the use of this drug. But it did not deter young women who had no wish to become pregnant. For the first time, if used properly, the pill, a product made from the pee of pregnant mares, could virtually free a woman from the fear of unwanted pregnancy. For men, it was a gift from the gods, as it moved the responsibility for contraception from the man to the woman. And we all know, when it comes to sexual relations with a woman, responsibility flies out of a man's sexual window.

The mid-twentieth century was a time when ordinary people spoke out against the evils of racial segregation, especially as practised in the old Confederate plantation states, and a time for protesting an unpopular war in Asia, when thousands of well-educated young Americans fled north on unfamiliar roads, leaving their homes and families to seek refuge, sanctuary, and permanent exile in Canada. This was a time when those elegant, predominantly European ocean liners that had connected continents by sea routes for over a century were unceremoniously torpedoed and sunk by the less elegant, more practical American-built Boeing and Douglas jetliners. It was a time when colour televisions slowly replaced the old flickering black and white, and the frozen TV dinner was invented to effortlessly heat and then consume while watching that new colour TV. It was a time of reel-to-reel tape decks and tiny eight-transistor radios, a time of the incredibly inspired "You meet the nicest people on a Honda" advertising campaign. It was a time of the cola wars. It was a time of the imprinting of American values and culture and American English upon the fabric of the Western world, values that made subtle, subversive intrusions, even penetrating the dull concrete-grey Soviet-dominated prison state of Eastern Europe, making them restless and yearn for freedom.

And speaking of dull and grey, even we, residing at the northern end of 1,000 kilometres of railway line in Churchill, were influenced by things American. It was inescapable and, more to the point, too decadent to avoid. First, we in Churchill were surrounded by Americans—servicemen and their families, hundreds of them. And those Americans packed their values in their suitcases, along with their cigarettes. Then we were hooked on Hollywood fantasy, a world of make-believe, tinsel, smoke, and mirrors, where Doris Day lived in an enormous house, as we imagined most Americans did, with a private swimming pool and a thing we had never seen called a "patio." Doris sang songs, mysteriously accompanied by a full orchestra, which apparently hid in a bedroom as we never saw even a trace of it, while she drifted, still singing, from room to room. We kids would studiously watch the movement of her lips to see if they actually moved in sync with the words being sung. And unfortunately for our cardiac health, we were fond of American-inspired fast food. "Cheeseburger and large fries, please, and a cola. Thanks." Heart attacks would come much later.

In the world blessed with TV, millions watched shows portraying the perfect American families, presided over by perfect parents with beautiful, perfect children. It was a world of *Leave It to Beaver*, *The Adventures of Ozzie and Harriet*, and *Father Knows Best*, and they left each of us wondering what was wrong with our own family. Girls then wore bobby socks, used bobby pins, and swooned over Bobby Vinton, Bobby Vee, or Bobby Darin. And we boys, like Brando or Dean, wore blue jeans with a T-shirt, preferably black with a soft pack of cigarettes pushed in a manly way into the left sleeve, and hair glued down with more than a dab of greasy hair cream.

We boys avoided discs recorded by one of the Bobbys and favoured those that were manly, and guitar driven, such as "Rebel Rouser" by Duane Eddy; or the throbbing, sexy pulse of "Teen Beat" by drummer Sandy Nelson; or Little Richard's frantic piano stylings with "Tutti Frutti."

For Canadians living in remote corners of the nation, or far enough from large cities and their resident department stores, the fashion links to the outside world were the catalogues, issued two or three times a year by the dominant Canadian retailers, the queen of which, in Canada, was Eaton's. The Eaton's catalogue was the retail bible, to be studied and pored over. It was a lifeline for my mother, who felt somewhat like a hostage in a community that, after all, offered little to the average housewife. Eaton's catalogues were, like her Harlequin Romance novels, one of her escapes from the reality of northern life.

There was an Eaton's outlet upstairs from the Royal Bank and the Maple Leaf Services grocery store in Fort Churchill. It was there that orders were taken, and products delivered, three times a week with the arrival of the train from Winnipeg. Larger items, like car tires, were to be personally picked up by the customer at the train station. I recall Mother buying me new shoes through the catalogue. She would choose a pair of sensible oxford shoes on page 98, item number XYZ123 BLACK. Then she would place my left foot and then my right foot on a piece of paper, draw the outline of each foot, take the piece of paper to the Eaton's catalogue outlet, and place the order to be sent to Winnipeg, where it would reach the Eaton's catalogue warehouse. Within a couple of weeks, my shoes were delivered, accompanied by the company mantra, "Goods satisfactory or money gladly refunded." The shoes were always satisfactory to my Mother—rarely to me—but she paid the bill. Her decision was final. I, however, would much rather have had the refund and kept the old pair of shoes.

My Mother shopped the goods artfully displayed within the pages of the Eaton's catalogue. There she discovered happy, carefree men, women, and children showing off the goods on offer. Smiling, obedient children, unnaturally clean from head to toe, wearing smart, well-fitting trousers, dresses, blouses, shorts, shoes, shirts, skirts, and sweaters. Well-groomed, handsome men stood in stiff poses, looking as if they were about to catch an invisible ball thrown by an invisible person. And the ladies—yes, the ladies—all, oh, so pretty, were to be worshipped from a safe distance, secretly away from our parents, especially when we delved into the pages illustrating ladies' underwear, or "intimate apparel" as it was artfully and slyly called. It seemed that after a month or two, the catalogue automatically opened at these pages, much to the consternation of mothers and the quiet, knowing nods of approval by fathers.

My Mother drooled over the wonderful world of appliances. Televisions, mostly black and white, and a few very expensive colour; combination radio-and-stereo record players and portables with "in-the-lid" speakers and records to play on them; refrigerators with storage capacity in the doors and plastic or aluminum ice cube trays to fit neatly into the freezer compartment; dishwashers; and two types of washing machines: "wringers," with rollers to squeeze out the water from clothing and, if careless, pull in and mangle the occasional finger or two, and the brand new, very expensive automatic washer. "Imagine that", Mum would mutter to herself. "A machine that washes, rinses, and spins so that the clothes are almost dry automatically." And dryers, so that all laundry could be completely, nicely dried. No more need for laundry lines in the backyard or base-ment. What a wonderful new American decade this was. All those devices, there to work at the push of a button. And to top it off, many of the fabrics produced by American mills were of "no-iron" fabric. Science gave us synthetic polyester, a new product that went from the washer to the hanger, a new man-made fabric that produced drip-dry, no-iron shirts, no-iron trousers, no-iron blouses and skirts, no-iron nighties. The fact that this wonderful new fabric would ignite and burn in a warm breeze was brushed aside. The catalogue from Eaton's promised repeatedly a wonderful new world lying within its pages, literally at the feet of those whose eyes feasted on the artfully displayed merchandise available "on easy monthly terms." And what a wonderful new world it was. It was a world where washing, drying, and ironing were banished from the housewife's daily routine, so that the harried housewife would have more time to watch the afternoon soap operas on that spanking-new colour television. However, because my Mother lived in the Churchill townsite in the 1950s, the promise of this new world, full of labour-saving devices for sale within the brightly coloured pages of the Eaton's catalogue, did not apply. Why not?

The answer lay in the town of Churchill itself. At the time, the town had no running water, no taps because there was no running water, no sewers, no flush toilets, no showers, no bathtubs, no drained paved roads, none of the basics one might have considered essential in a town as large as Churchill. Reliable electrical power outlets didn't arrive until the late 1950s. So what use were those wonderful automatic machines that could wash and spin and dry all those labour-saving no-iron shirts, skirts, and dresses if there were no sewage systems or municipal water supply?

When we first moved to Churchill, we lived in a tiny, rented house situated behind the local theatre and beside the Pentecostal church. So you can see, we lived in the middle of the action. It didn't take me long to discover the bowling alley, as that was also the location of the local pool hall, a place I was forbidden by my Father to patronize. On the other hand, unlike my Mother, a soul with a deep spiritual side, I avoided the neighbouring tabernacle whenever possible. I felt uncomfortable with the arm waving, done as if to invite the angelic host to come crashing in through the ceiling, amid cries of "Praise the Lord!" and "Hallelujah!"

I soon made friends at school, and our first stop after school on leaving the bus in the town square was to head for the forbidden fruit, the pool hall and bowling alley. Inside, a jukebox blared the latest selections from the hit parade, both pop and country, and the place was blue with cigarette smoke, alive with the roll and rumble of bowling balls speeding down one or more of the four 8-pin lanes, or the steady "click-click" of pool balls on one or more of the three tables. For a fifteen-year-old, this was a wonderful place, a sort of Aladdin's cave where Ali Baba and the forty thieves hung out.

Around quarter after five, before my old man returned home from work, I wandered out of the alley toward the place my family called home. It was far removed from the glossy photos found in the catalogues or Doris Day's magnificent home in the movies, complete with pool and patio. However, I must say that Dad did his best. Like most things one took for granted in the balmy south, housing was in short supply in the north. You took what was on offer.

Our house was a house in name only. It had four walls, a roof, some windows, and one front—or was it a back door? This depended upon one's perspective as to which part of the house was in fact the front or back. Current health and safety regulations would prohibit chickens roosting in it, let alone permit human habitation. There were two tiny bedrooms, one for my parents, and the other I shared with my younger and therefore much ignored brother. The bedrooms had no windows and no doors. Mother quickly ran together a pair of curtains for privacy. There was a small living room-cum-dining room with two sets of frosty leaky windows and, facing the pool hall and theatre, a porch-like passage ran the length of the house. At one end was the only door out, and at the other end, near the kitchen, was the toilet. This passage housed the large water barrel that was filled weekly. The house, to say the least, was a fire trap, and the situation of the toilet, a risk to our health. The toilet was just big enough to do one's business, with only a curtain made by my mother for privacy. This tiny toilet had no sink, no water, no flush, no heat—just a steel container, complete with a handle nestled within a larger steel container that was fitted with a seat and lid. It often fell to me, as the older boy, to remove and empty the inner container with the handle before the contents spilled over. I would carefully carry the container out to a wooden crib in the backyard and dispose of the loathsome contents into a hole. It was awesomely medieval. As I didn't, in my youth, expire from some horrible pestilence, I was probably protected from future plagues for life. Once the bucket was emptied, I replaced the wooden lid on the crib and then tried to manoeuvre myself back to the house while carrying the empty bucket without slipping or falling over. This process was difficult at the best of times, but I defy anybody not to slip a little and splash a little, especially when the temperature made walking difficult. Children today raised on soaps that kill 99.9 percent of germs would keel over just by looking at a picture of our bathroom facilities.

And speaking of bathrooms, our bathtub was a round, galvanized steel tub that we partially filled with hot water from the hot water reservoir at the end of the stove. Thus, the kitchen (the warmest room in the house) was also our bathroom. Needless to say, we bathed once a week, a great treat usually reserved for Sunday evenings. The grey water was then carefully poured into the sink where it disappeared down the drain, down a pipe that ran through the floor, and once free of the confines of the pipe, meandered wherever it wished beneath the house until, in winter at least, it froze into mounds of ice that cascaded toward the outside world, much to my fascination.

Just as the sun is the source of life on earth, the stove was the source of life in our house. It was our furnace, our cooking device, our reservoir of hot water, and when I say "our," I really mean my Mother's. She was responsible for cooking, making hot beverages, bathing us, baking, and making sure that the contraption kept on working. The stove was an old-fashioned cast iron appliance that, even by the 1950s, had seen decades of yeoman service. Originally, the stove was fuelled by coal or wood, but ours ignored precedent. It had been, I am convinced, illegally modified into an oil burner, much like oil-burning space heaters that were common at the time. If memory correctly serves me, and here it may be a bit wonky, I recall Dad lighting a pan located at the rear of the stove and then switching on a fan that blew a jet-like tongue of flame into the space where the foresaid wood or coal would have been burning. The result, for a boy of fifteen, was spectacular and, I am now convinced, was then, and would be now, light years away from any building code. But Churchill in the 1950s couldn't care less about codes of any description. The town was a code-free free-for-all. Fires did happen, but that was the price paid for any lack of enforcement of even basic regulation. It was a world of "every man for himself." And the stove itself, with coaxing from Mother, delivered our hot meals and hot water, and was the only defence against the −30°C temperature outside. And I am positive that my old man never bothered with fire insurance. It was probably never offered by any sensible insurance company that wished to remain in business anyway.

Mum washed our clothes, not in a spanking new automatic washer delivered by Eaton's but in a well-used wringer washer that Dad bought second-hand. Churchill was a very transient community, and the opportunities to purchase the flotsam of those leaving was continuous. Dad was a great scrounger and bought most of our stuff second-hand, including beds, tables and chairs, couches, side tables and lamps, and his beloved '57 Ford Ranchero. While living at home, attending school locally, I only saw my old man purchase two new things. The first was a stereophonic radio and record player that he called a "radiogram," and the second, a Japanese made reel-to-reel stereophonic tape deck. I was forbidden to touch either, except to turn on the radio in the evening so that he could listen to the 6:00 p.m. news if reception permitted. Sometimes, we received no new news for days. The amazing thing about my old man was that he loved his opera and classical music as much as Mum loved Johnny Mathis or Nat King Cole. He even joined a record club (purchase your first ten for one cent) so that he could listen into the evening on a cold winter's night. He was a tradesman with the soul of a poet.

Our water was delivered once a week by the "waterman," Jules—a French Canadian—short in stature, swarthy, and strong as an ox, wearing a parka and a pair of enormous sheepskin-lined boots. He never knocked. He announced his arrival by banging the door open and hauling a heavy hose behind him that was attached to his truck. The hose was hoisted to the top of the large steel barrel located in the back porch, and the water, our water for a whole week, was pumped in. Jules was then paid according to the volume of water he delivered. The barrel had a tap at the base. Gravity allowed for water to flow from the tap to a bucket, and the water was then carried to the reservoir on the stove.

The back porch, where the tank was located, was always cold in winter and was just warm enough to prevent the drum from freezing solid, although in mid-winter, we did often have an inch or two of ice forming on the top of the water.

When it was really cold, my old man would hang a kerosene-fuelled hurricane lamp in the toilet so that that our bottom ends didn't stick to the seat. At times, when it was freezing cold, you didn't want to go there. You postponed your visit to the toilet and only went to do your business when you really had to. So, in a nutshell, you didn't enjoy the experience.

We lived for two years in that house beside the Pentecostal church and then suddenly moved. The second house was larger, and in most respects nicer to live in, but I knew I would miss the Sunday performance in the church next door. How the spirit moved those folks was a constant source of wonder to me, although I must confess, I never felt the urge to join in on the "angel-calling" arm-waving exercise. No, not in the least!

Our new house, we soon discovered, floated according to the season. In winter, the floor and walls would part company, leaving a gap of several centimetres, and in summer, the walls would separate from the ceiling, and the space would close on the floor. It, too, was drafty, especially around window frames and through electrical outlets. Condensation froze on the windows, especially in the kitchen and my bedroom, and in idle moments I would try to melt the ice by pressing my fingers against it. The heat from those fingers usually proved to be insufficient.

There were two separate bedrooms, a living room, and a combination kitchen and diner where I did my homework on the kitchen table. Each bedroom and the living room exited onto the kitchen, where there could be found a brown, oil-fired Eatonia Viking space heater, which occasionally went out, as well as a propane-fuelled gas stove. Both the oil tank and propane tank were outside, near the kitchen and my bedroom window, and when it was intensely cold, the propane wanted to remain in its liquid form rather than turn into a gas. This presented some problems to my mother, who resorted to feeding us sandwiches on those extra cold days, as cooking was quite impossible.

A small toilet and two—yes, two—water tanks were in the porch. Oh, the luxury! Water was now abundant! And, although the toilet facilities were similar to our first house, the new house had a sink—no taps but a sink and plug—and one could wash one's hands while admiring one's reflection in a mirror on the wall. And, after admiring oneself and the washing of the hands, the plug was pulled from the sink, and the water would disappear down a hole. I gave little thought to where, as I knew. And as a plus, the room had a window. What a huge step for mankind. Mind you, there was the same kind of toilet as before, sometimes referred to as a "chemical toilet," although I have no idea why.

The bedroom I slept in faced the prevailing wind, and a huge snowbank would form in front of the window. It was a cold room at the best of times. I recall on winter mornings, waking up and hearing the wind howling outside. Sitting up, I then found my bedding frozen to the wall, especially around the electrical outlet.

On one school-day morning, still sleepy at seven o'clock, I dressed in jeans and a shirt and made my way to the kitchen. The Eatonia Viking heater was working, and I sleepily put my elbow on the top of it and laid my head down. I was tired after all. Suddenly, my old man began hitting my back. To say I was put off was an understatement, until I realized that my wonderful

American-made, no-iron, drip-dry, polyester fabric shirt purchased from the catalogue had somehow come into contact with an open flame of the propane stove and had begun to cremate itself instantly! Funny thing, initially I felt nothing of the fire. I was also wearing a T-shirt, and it, too, had escaped the flame. I was unaware that I was a human torch. My old man grinned, called me a few choice names, and I knew nothing more would be said once I was flame free. I was lucky beyond words.

I must refer to one more momentous event that occurred in our second home in Churchill. It was Sunday, and my old man was sleeping on the boxy, grey-upholstered, very '50s couch in the living room, his head on one arm of the couch, his inexplicably bare feet hanging over the other. It was around noon on a Sunday and, after all, a day of rest. He deserved the time as his shop was open for five full days a week and a half day on Saturday. Dad did not often attend church, mostly just weddings and funerals. He would tell me that if you followed the teachings of the Bible and lived a good life, God would take you in before he took in many of the hypocrites that regularly attended church. However, on that particular Sunday, he probably should have joined the hypocrites in church and taken Mother with him too! Alas, he stayed home, as did Mother, who, in a usual state of giddiness, had tickled his nose as she walked by. Dad made a slapping motion at Mum's hand, and she then ran off. She quickly rounded the end of the couch, where Dad's feet lay, toes vertical, and she headed in the direction of the kitchen. The next thing she did we debated and, when Dad was not within earshot, giggled at for years. It was chewed over and over, enjoyed like a good meal. Mum grabbed Dad's left big toe, probably for balance as she rounded the couch, and, unfortunately, did not let go as the toe twisted. All I can say is that Dad howled, Mum stopped in horror, and we all realized she had done something really awful.

It was at the hospital where we found that (a) Dad had indeed broken a toe, (b) nothing could be done to mend a broken toe, (c) he would not walk without considerable pain for weeks, and (d) he would be confined to home, using his sick leave, because he could not wear work boots. To his credit, my Dad stuck it out at home for as long as he could. But he felt like a rudderless ship, drifting in an unfamiliar sea. And he hated sick leave. He, in his quirky way, equated sick leave as a form of welfare that shirkers took, not as something he had earned and was entitled to. Staying home, hobbling around as Mother busied herself around the house, was more than he could bear. Not that he didn't love Mother. He really did. But like all good things we dream about, a limit can be reached, like eating chocolate to excess. Finally, in an act of desperation, he returned to work wearing slippers.

And although at the time he saw nothing amusing in living with the inconvenience of a broken big toe, after Mum passed, he looked back through the softened rosy lens of time and could crack a smile. Mother, we all knew, could be giddy. "Addle-headed" was how my Dad put it. He would then smile, and we knew just how much he missed her.

SAVE THE LAST DANCE FOR ME

As a child in Sunday school, I had been told the story of creation, had been credibly informed by earnest people who knew of Adam and Eve, of how they lived and romped in their birthday suits in a paradise called "Eden," and how Eve had tempted Adam with the forbidden fruit—an apple—and how he took a bite. With that, things went terribly wrong! Lions no longer slept with lambs; they ate them! And Adam and Eve and their children and their children's children modestly hid their naughty bits with clothes, resulting in the long run as a boon for fashion designers and an anchor attached to one's wallet. And as for the apple story, it really didn't register with me. After all, I was told by my Mother, who in those childhood years I believed without question, to eat apples; they were good for me. In fact, I quite liked apples, and along with my cousin Charlie, as small boys in the idyllic English countryside of Hampshire, we picked basketfuls from our granny's tree.

Yes, it was indeed a strange biblical story until, that is, my hormones awakened and bloomed around thirteen. Then it registered. Girls were, like Eve, made to tempt and tease and terrify a boy who had just grown a herd of hormones, who began to speak with a strange deep voice, and, most alarmingly, found hair in places other than the top of his head. Girls were soft and round and sweet and perfumed. Boys were not! Boys were gawky, awkward, grubby, disorganized, noisy, surly, and clumsy. By fifteen, I was captivated. Girls, I discovered, were charming and alluring in a "girly" sense, and as the French remind us in their quaint, "*Oh là la*," Gallic way, "*Vive la différence!*" Yes, comparing a boy of fifteen to a girl of fifteen is like comparing chalk to cheese. And like a magnet to steel, I was attracted. My rush of newly minted, shiny hormones saw to that. My mind in idle moments would wander, and I found myself daydreaming about girls, taking secretive sly glances at girls, talking about girls for hours with my friends, and even having short-lived crushes on girls—crushes that could shift abruptly; such is the fickle mind of a fifteen-year-old. Very little in the mind of a fifteen-year-old even suggests permanence of any kind.

And like most fifteen-year-old boys, I was shy and tongue-tied in the company of a girl. The fine art of conversation is a learned one, and I, at fifteen, had learned little. My talking points certainly needed polishing. I, for example, liked war films, westerns, and John Wayne. Most girls did not. They liked pop stars named Tommy or Bobby, and the latest in fashion. I was interested in neither. I enjoyed fishing, but most girls squirmed with the flopping around of a live fish, and they certainly would never, ever, ever touch that slimy thing! Consequently, the process of asking a girl out on a date was, for a tongue-tied lad like me, about as easy as Edmund Hillary ascending Mount Everest for the first time in 1953. In fact, it was probably easier for him as he had help from his Nepalese Sherpa, Tenzing Norgay.

On whom could I call for help? My old man? Get real. Absolutely not! My Mother? Oh, come on now. Get serious! I was alone on that mountain, the air was frigid and thin, and the only way up was to wind up my courage and reach for the top. The summit awaited me.

In the late 1950s when I was young, there were no cellphones to call a girl from wherever you happened to be. As a matter of fact, I was young long before many of the things we now take for granted were available. No iPads, no self-parking cars, no microwave ovens, no tubeless tires, no seatbelts in cars, no open-heart surgery, no frost-free refrigerators, no bottled water, no area nor postal codes, no smoke-free premises, no diet cola, no unleaded gasoline. The list goes on and on.

Does this mean I lived an empty life? Of course not! How can one miss something they never had? My life was full to the brim. For example, my television was a radio, a device with absolutely no picture whatsoever! Right?

We did, like most, have a telephone in our house. It was black. As a matter of fact, they were all black, as heavy as a cast-iron pot, with a dial, and attached to the wall with a length of cable wire. The handset, connected to the body of the phone by a length of black plastic-covered coiled wire, had a nasty habit of getting its coils all wrapped up on each other, sometimes making it all but impossible to sit any more than three feet from the phone while using it to make a call. Also, to further complicate the issue, many phones, including ours, were on a party line. For those of you who don't know, a party line was one telephone line shared by two or more phones in two or more homes with different rings to identify who was to answer the phone. This meant that nosy neighbours could, and often did, listen in to private conversations and were the source of local gossip. "Mrs. Smith, I can hear you breathing. Don't pretend you're not there. Please get off the phone," was a frequent request. And this was the device, usually in full view and earshot of the entire family, a boy used to ask out a young lady on a Friday evening. And to make matters worse, the girl's family phone was usually in a similar location in her household, often answered by her father, who had handed the handset over to his daughter, who was then probably subjected to an inquisition once the call had ended. Privacy was a concept not yet thought of. About the only place one could safely be alone with one's thoughts was in the one and only toilet in the house, where one could be left to contemplate in solitude until somebody else wanted to use the facility. I do believe my very real phobia of and antipathy toward the telephone began at this time. Even today, in my approaching dotage, I still hate using the telephone and will only very reluctantly answer.

There was, of course, a second and equally public way of attempting a possible date with a young lady, and that was to approach her in the school hallway, near her locker, where other students, friends, foes, and the indifferent alike were milling about close by. Boys who chose this method were paddling in water fraught with danger, and the whole effort could, regretfully, rapidly deteriorate into a gossip's meal for a week or more.

On the other hand—because convention never encouraged her to directly ask a boy out, except, that is, on Sadie Hawkins Day, a day now relegated to the dustbin of history—a girl would be forced to use a more complex and convoluted method of getting a boy's attention, a boy on whom, for that week, she had a serious crush.

The third and preferred method was that the girl would ask a trusted friend, a confidant, someone who was willing to speak for her and represent her, to begin the process. This trusted friend was a modern example of a medieval king's herald. Thus, a girl might send out a signal through her friend to another girl who was a friend of the girlfriend of a boy who was, coincidentally, the friend of the boy who was a best friend of the boy she was interested in. Ultimately, the objective was to telegraph with enough accuracy through the verbal maze so that it would give the chosen boy the green light to ask her out—that is, if he deemed her to be cute and have straight teeth, and he understood the concept of green lights.

However, the reality for us boys was that we were usually dateless. To compensate, we saw ourselves as lone wolves, alpha wolves who stood free and independent. At least this is what we told ourselves. It was a good excuse, and it was all nonsense of course. Truthfully, most weekends found us in an exclusive male-only club, where the talk of girls and our exploits with girls far exceeded reality. But hope springs eternal, and we lived in a constant state of hope. We were, after all, fifteen-year-olds at the bottom of the pecking order, not yet old enough to drive legally. And it did appear that those guys of sixteen or seventeen who by virtue of their age could drive, or those who had quit school and were, in our estimation, making huge paycheques and had purchased a car, had a huge advantage. Girls, I then believed, were impressed by one of two things, neither of which I possessed: money and cars. And those guys often had both. It was not fair, but that was the way it was.

There were two Friday attractions that allowed us boys to enjoy limited access to members of the opposite sex. The first was to attend the early showing of the movie at The Garrison, the local movie theatre. There, for the price of admission, fifteen cents, we watched the world unroll on the screen before us, at least the world as Hollywood saw it. There we saw westerns, war stories, horror tales, and historical pageants; a succession of Elvis Presley films, which were just a vehicle for his songs; and a multitude of beach-romp, romance, song-and-dance, surfboarding productions. Girls clad in bikinis bounced around on the beach, especially Annette Funicello and Sandra Dee. The male stars, usually named Troy or Frankie, were the object of much derision.

We boys always sat in a group a couple of rows behind the gaggle of giggling girls, who knew we were there and did their best to pretend to ignore us. These girls were in Grades 8 or 9, they were around fourteen or fifteen years old, and all apparently shopped from the same catalogue, as they not only dressed similarly to the pictures of the girls in the catalogue but also wore their hair in the same way. Ponytails were "in," as were white blouses and baby blue or pink sweaters. Skirts were, regretfully, pre-minis and fell below the knee by a modest two or three inches, although I am sure the fathers would have preferred they be at least ankle length but yielded to their daughters' sense of fashion. To complete the look, the girls tied silky white scarves delicately around their necks.

In complete contrast, we boys appeared to work very hard to look rough and tough. The catalogue had little influence on our fashion sense, but Marlon Brando and James Dean certainly did. There is a wonderful expression: "In the flower of their lout hood." And we were, believe me, in full bloom—the recurring nightmare of any girl's father, if one of us showed up at his door to escort his "little girl" out on a date.

Our hair was generously slicked down, and we struggled our lean and lank legs into tight blue jeans. We completed the look with black T-shirts and windbreakers. This was our signature "He's a rebel" look.

None of us would ever wear penny loafers, tan-coloured pleated slacks, or button-down plaid shirts, which would have been a dreamy attire if our mothers had their way. If, by chance, there had been an appearance by any one of us in those togs, there would have been an incredulous "What the fuck you wearin'?" response from my friends, followed by a shameful shunning until the condemned smartened up. After all, you have to look cool to be cool, and we thought ourselves the epitome of cool.

Thus, in the darkened theatre, Hollywood would flicker its vision of America upon the screen, always accompanied, of course, by the mandatory Bugs Bunny or Wile E. Coyote cartoon, as well as the newsreels, which were always at least one or two weeks late—newsreels where we got to see what Kennedy or Khrushchev looked like in black and white.

Then around eight o'clock, the movie ended as Annette kissed Frankie on some warm, sandy California beach, and the lights of the theatre would go up. Out we went, and if nothing else was happening, we'd head upstairs to play pool or devour a cheeseburger with fries and a large fountain cola. Sometimes we'd walk to Doug's house to perhaps turn on his dad's black-and-white TV to see if anything appeared on the screen, as it did occasionally. On a couple of occasions, we did receive freak transmissions of US stations but only briefly. If the evening was warm enough, we'd head to the rocks and perhaps light a fire and talk about Annette running around in her bikini.

There was, however, during the winter, held once or twice a month after the movie, a tortuous sort of affair for a fifteen-year-old boy, called the "Teen Dance." It did, to be truthful, keep us off the streets and out of trouble for a couple of hours, and it was probably the only parentally approved event where the boys and girls could meet and, if dancing, albeit briefly, could touch each other inches apart, as they shuffled awkwardly around the floor to the sound of Brenda Lee sobbing her heart out as she repeated, "I'm sorry, so sorry."

There were always chaperones at these dances: a small group of anxious, nervous mothers, who perhaps remembered these kinds of dances in their youth, and a tribe of warrior fathers, who certainly remembered these kinds of dances when they were young. The fathers' objectives were simple: to make sure their daughters only danced, preferably with another girl!

The odd thing about these chaperones was that rarely did the parents of boys seem interested in chaperoning these dances. In that vein, my parents never bothered.

By nine o'clock in the evening, the sixteen- and seventeen-year-old boys had, by reason of their maturity, worldliness, money, and driving licences, cornered many of the pretty and available fifteen- and sixteen-year-old girls, who were obviously in awe of the boys' self-assurance, leaving the rest of us boys to stand transfixed, like sweaty statues, in a line along the wall, facing the unclaimed girls, who were standing huddled in small groups along the opposite wall.

And there between us, like a void as deep and as wide as the Grand Canyon, was the floor we younger boys would be forced to traverse if we summoned enough courage to ask a young lady for a dance. In simple psychological terms, this presented a classic "approach-avoidance" situation. The reward, a "yes" from a girl followed by an awkward turn around the dance floor, was a confirmation of one's sense of manhood. A refusal was too horrible to contemplate—a walk back to the dark side, to the other boys lining the wall, with every eyeball in the room, you were convinced, on you and watching you. A refusal was far too painful to even think of. A refusal was, beyond a doubt, the very worst thing that could damage and dent the ego of a boy of fifteen. Boys of fifteen really do bruise easily, despite the "couldn't give a shit anyway" veneer, a veneer made up of bravado and little else.

However, a simple nod by a girl—that "I Want to Hold Your Hand" moment—meant three whole minutes of holding a girl or shuffling around the floor with her. And once Johnny had completed his breathless "Twelfth of Never," you and she awkwardly parted, and with a grin of victory, you, like the conquering Caesar, returned victoriously to the company of those losers who still leaned awkwardly against the wall of the hall.

The climax of any teen dance was always the last dance, announced with relief by a male-parent chaperone. The last dance was always a slow dance. As the strains of the music filled the hot, hormone-laden air, the race to find a partner still standing along her side of the hall was set in motion. And if you had the nerve, and if you were lucky, the girl nodded, and the last dance commenced.

No great skill was required to slow dance. All you needed to do with your partner was a sort of shuffle around the floor, as some singer named Bobby or Tommy filled the air with a suitable noise. And if you were lucky, the girl moved in close; if you were not, you and the girl resembled a set of awkwardly moving chopsticks, holding each other as far as possible apart, yet still moving in unison. The former was great fun—the latter, not so much.

With the music fading, the boy and girl awkwardly disengaged—she to join her friends and then return home to very relieved parents, no doubt, and he to find his friends to gloat and compare notes. As for me and my friends, we boys would troop off, pushing each other, shouting noisily, laughing, and celebrating life so newly discovered. In the meantime, before events in life caught up with us, as they are wont to do, we hurried off. The last bus home was waiting.

EAT, DRINK, AND BE MERRY!

When I was a teenaged, self-obsessed lout, I thought little about the quality and variety of the meals my Mother successfully and routinely brought to the table, day after day, month after month, year after year. The plates appeared around six o'clock in the evening. My brother, Father, and I sat down at our appointed places around that table, and we ate what was put in front of us. I suspect this same repetitive process was played out in countless homes throughout the land. It seemed to me to be a remarkably simple process. But I was to discover that simple, it simply wasn't.

Today at home, I cook many of our meals, not because I have an overly generous spirit, but, more selfishly, if I wait for my ever-loving missus to return from her labours and prepare a meal, we won't eat until eight o'clock—and that quite simply will not do. So, I cook. Or attempt to. The diet that I have created is repetitive and depends an awful lot on stuff found frozen in plastic bags or boxes, with directions like, "Preheat oven to 500 degrees and cremate." However, my wife never complains, bless her heart. She, as I did, many years ago, eats the stuff put on the plate in front of her. It may not be haute cuisine and will fail the taste buds of those obnoxious chefs that abound on the television, but it is, indeed, a meal made with love.

However, and here I must emphasize this, there is a big difference between what my Mother prepared and what I prepare because of the availability and the quality of basic raw materials. I am now able to purchase the ingredients that are the foundation of our meals. No matter the season, I am surrounded by competing markets that are jammed with an assortment of local and distantly shipped fresh fruits, produce, meats derived from a veritable zoo of animals, frozen stuff in plastic bags, frozen stuff in boxes, breads, buns, milk from cows and goats, and drinkable products apparently made from almonds or soy that remarkably taste like chocolate milk. And almost everything has a "Best Before" date stamped on it.

As I am a person on a pension, I often look for and purchase products close to the end of their "Best Before" date because I figure that if the food I ate when I was a teenager didn't kill me then—and most of that stuff would have been at or even well beyond the "Best Before" date, if there had been a "Best Before" date stamped on the product, which there wasn't—then this stuff today won't kill me either. And it's usually 50 percent off! And, even better, purchasing 50-percent-off products on one of the monthly "Customer Appreciation Days" or "Seniors' Days," which offers a further 10 percent off everything, including the 50 percent off "Best Before" products, means head-spinning financial rewards. Bargains galore!

My Mother had none of these advantages. No "Best Before" date. No 50 percent off. No 10 percent off. And as for frozen food in plastic sealed bags—nope! Pre-made frozen pies? Nope. Again, never saw one. Fresh vegetables? Maybe, but usually not so fresh. Lettuce, even in season, was wilted and often brown—tomatoes, soft and unappealing. And tomatoes and lettuce were prohibitively expensive. Yes, prices were high; quality, low; and salads, nonexistent.

Cabbages and potatoes were the two fresh products that had the best chance of surviving the long rail trip north, but in general, we ate mostly canned or dried vegetables. Canned peas, dried peas, canned green beans, dried green beans, dried white beans, canned brown beans, canned waxed vegetables, but never, ever canned spinach, despite Popeye's claim it made him strong. My old man hated spinach, and that, as they say, was that. And canned corn was also not one of his favourites. But Mum liked corn, so she defied him and bought it and served it, placing the kernels on her plate and on our plates but never on my old man's. He referred to corn as "chicken food." His disdain for corn was limitless. Yes, he had an irrational hatred for corn.

On one memorable occasion that was written into family folklore, Mother prepared a stew from the usual ingredients: cubed stewing beef—retrieved from our freezer, which was better known to all others as "the attic"—carrots, onions, canned tomatoes, bouillon cubes, and for some obscure reason, she emptied a can of whole kernel corn into the bubbling mixture. She, as was often the case, was probably worlds away, perhaps waltzing with Johnny Mathis as he crooned "Twelfth of Never," and simply not thinking as she opened and emptied the can. Mother, you see, understandably tended to survive the harsh reality of the north by escaping, in her mind, to another place, to another world. Thus, she danced in Johnny's ballroom or read her romantic novels, where a bare-chested hero swept his beloved off her feet. To be honest, when the stew was served on my plate, along with boiled potatoes, dumplings, and chunks of fresh homemade bread, I was indifferent to the corn and appreciated the warm glow of the rich aroma floating up and saying "yum" beneath my nose. Dad, on the other hand, sat there and stared at his plate. There was obviously no "yum" floating beneath his nose at all. He glared at the stew, then looked at Mum, who had probably spent much of the afternoon making the stew, reading racy Harlequin Romance novels, baking bread, listening to some sort of lady's hour on the radio, and dancing with Johnny Mathis as he crooned. She was tired, missed her chain-smoking, unruly tribe of a rural English family, and was a wee bit cranky. But Dad, as it turned out, was crankier. Hard work in a confined space does that to a man. "What's this?" he demanded, looking at the few kernels of canned corn that were floating between the dumplings on the surface of the stew. He then stared at Mother. And then, the *coup de grâce*. The wrong thing to say at the wrong time. Out came the words, "Chicken food!" These, it turned out, were the atomic bomb of wrong words to say to a tired lady. Dancing with Johnny will do this to you.

As I have said, Mother could be cranky, but she was usually a woman of infinite patience. She had to be to put up with this. I had rarely seen her patience break until then. She calmly rose from her chair. Only her eyes spoke with how very angry she was. We all watched, transfixed in breathless anticipation. What next? My eyes switched from her to Dad and back to her. She squeezed herself between me and the wall behind me and then stood, angry but controlled, beside the old man, who always occupied the king's chair at the king's spot at the head of the table. The king was obviously in trouble. The serf, it appeared, was now in full rebellion. A smart king at this moment would try to save his crown, negotiate with the rebel, pour oil on troubled waters. He didn't. She picked up the offending plate, complete with boiled potatoes and dumplings, put a couple of chunks of her freshly baked crusty bread on top of the stew, and appeared as if she were about to remove the plate from the table. She then—as we boys watched, wide-eyed—walked behind the old man, plate in hand, lifted the plate, and then reversed it over his head. Nobody moved. Nobody spoke. The only motion was the stew running down Dad's face and neck, down onto his shirt, and then onto the floor. Mother, as if in horror of what she had done, recoiled, and then stepped back.

The old man, breathing deeply, stood up, glared, but said nothing. Then he made his way past Mother and up the stairs. The silence was deafening. And like the teenage louts we were, with no sense at all, my brother and I just sat there in silence.

Mother sat down and cried, with the empty plate on the table, then wearily shook her teary-eyed head as if in denial of what she had done. She then pushed back the chair and followed Dad up the stairs. We heard words in the washroom, and then the voices moved into the bedroom and were muffled. My brother and I still did not move or speak.

On the brighter side, I might say that after that incident, Dad ate what was put in front of him with no comments, no "chicken food" reviews on the menu of the day. No! After that, all was well around the Horner table, although I did notice that if corn managed to make its way onto the old man's plate, he quickly and without comment simply pushed the offending kernels aside.

The meat from Mother's stew came from a cow Dad and some of his cronies purchased annually from a farmer who resided somewhere in the balmy south. Dad and company would buy the cow, have it murdered, dissected, and divided up into the cuts they wanted. The poor old cow, whether she wanted to or not, was coming to Churchill via the CN and would be delivered frozen, to be picked up by one of the cronies in his half-ton. The meat, all neatly wrapped in brown butchers' paper, was also neatly labelled: "four pounds chuck," "three pounds T-bone," "four pounds sirloin," "ten pounds hamburger." There were usually three or four people responsible for booking the meat, including the old man, and they would divide up exactly what was ordered. Incredibly, it always worked out. Once the division was completed, the meat made its way to each individual's house.

Now, strange as this may sound to modern ears, freezers were not common in the '50s, and even less common in Churchill. We certainly did not own one. But Churchill's climate could be counted on to provide nature's freezer, and the attics were the storage units.

Attics know two seasons. Hot in the summer. Going into an attic in August is almost guaranteed to give anyone heat exhaustion. And, in winter, the reverse. "Cold enough," the old man would say, "to freeze the nuts off a brass monkey." Thus, from late October to early May, we utilized the power of nature to keep our meat in a glacial state. I was often sent up to the attic opening to look for the cut Mum required. Once it was located and lowered through the hole and into the kitchen, the name of the cut was neatly crossed off the list kept in a drawer. She would demand hamburger for soup, cubed beef for stew, T-bones for special occasions. I needed a flashlight, or a "torch" as Mother insisted on calling it, in order to read the labelling on the packages and step carefully onto the beams. The old man had cut a four-by-eight sheet of plywood to size so that he could pass the pieces up to the attic hole and have me up there to lay the pieces on the beams. The meat was then placed in no particular order onto the plywood. Once up in the attic, my biggest fear was putting a foot through the ceiling or, even worse, falling through.

Mother never climbed the ladder to see the meat for herself, as she was notoriously unsteady on her feet when standing elevated on a chair or ladder looking for something in a cupboard just slightly higher than her head. To further illustrate this, Mother terrified my wife, Valerie, and me while tottering on an ancient wooden kitchen chair at our cottage in 1970, looking in a cupboard for something successfully hiding from her. She toppled over backward, her feet parting company with the chair. Back she fell, her head barely missing the stove and counter but landing, BANG, headfirst on the floor. We both momentarily feared she was dead. And there we were, alone, in a cottage, in the woods, miles from a hospital. But then, miraculously, she moved and began to breathe heavily. Her eyes flickered open, and she let out a groan. She was alive! But had she damaged her neck? Her head? The floor? The answer, thank goodness, was no. After a short while, she was up and about and appeared just as scatterbrained as she always was. She was, after all, a descendant of rural folk who had survived the Romans, Saxons, Vikings, Normans, a civil war between the king and parliament, the Dutch, the Spaniards, the French, the Germans, and whatever warlike gang had tried to tame them.

When it came to our diet and her innovative spirit, my Mother liked to experiment. She would take a basic recipe and modify it, putting a new twist on it. Sometimes she was successful and bathed in a glow of praise; sometimes, not. Like many English people, she battered and fried fish. It was deep-fried delicious. Then sometimes, playing with the ingredients, she would open a tin of canned ham or corned beef, cut it into thick slices, dip the slices in batter, and drop them carefully into a fryer. The result? Delicious! I loved it. My friends loved it. Even my dad loved it. Heart smart? Of course not! A steady diet of this would guarantee an early cardiac-arrested death. But, there again, the concept of good fats or bad fats was an unknown to those of her generation or mine. To her, a brick of lard was a basic cooking tool. And she fed us bread loaded with the solidified white drippings from a beef roast, onto which we liberally sprinkled layers of salt. She made bacon and eggs and then fried bread slices in the bacon fat. This we ate with relish, with two fried eggs reclining on the crispy, bacon fat–infused bread and three or four slices of bacon used as garnish around the plate. This meal was heavenly, unfortunately in more than one way. I am sure that if my good wife had continued in my mother's footsteps, with the delicious Sunday morning tradition, I would have pegged out and grown wings to fly with the angelic host many years ago.

Chicken was scarce in my home. I have no idea why. The highest compliment I heard as a child was for my grandmother to say, "My, that was delicious. It tasted just like chicken." Yes, chicken was regarded as haute cuisine in our household, an entree apparently reserved only for the royal family, for the rich and the famous. Consequently, almost every one of our meals consisted not of chicken but some kind of red meat or awful inner organ, which Mother boiled, broiled, fried, baked, roasted, or grilled, and always cooked so that the merest trace of red was banished. The question, "How well-done would you like the . . .?" (Insert any part of an animal here) was a question never asked. I then believed that all meat had to be cooked to dark brown or dry, and my family assumed that all civilized people wanted their beef or liver to be the consistency of leather boot soles. Medium rare was never an option offered. This cooking method was also true of vegetables. The concept of eating raw vegetables was incomprehensible. Cabbage, for example, had to acquire the same loose, slippery, limp texture as seaweed. The only exceptions were carrots, which I stole from the chopping block before Mother's knife cut the ends off my fingers. Cooking vegetables consisted of dropping them into boiling, well-salted water until done and then adding five minutes just to make sure they were well and truly dead. Only then were the meat and accompanying vegetables considered to be ready for the plate.

And we boys had one more enemy in the food department, one that was universally hated, except for the old man. He loved curry. But it was not curry in the Indian restaurant butter chicken kind of way. It was horrible, and I do not use the word lightly. Mother would make a delicious, "yum" inspired kind of stew and then when it was finished and ready to serve, add the old man's truly despicable radioactive green-yellow curry powder. When curry was the entree for the evening, Dad was pleased. I, on the other hand, would gag with each attempted spoonful and fill up with Mum's homemade bread.

To further complicate the culinary problems of the housewives in the local area, goods were shipped in, usually by rail, adding to the basic cost, making any perishable item two, three, or even four times the southern price. We only occasionally ate whole fresh potatoes because of their high cost or poor quality. And we never, ever drank fresh milk, as it was always expensive, rarely fresh, and often sour. Consequently, Mother plied us with powdered milk, which I reluctantly consumed, urged on because Mother said it was good for my teeth and bones. She must have been right as I still have most of my teeth and, at last count, all my bones. The milk I much preferred was canned evaporated milk, which I understand is like single malt Scotch, an acquired taste. I loved it and used it liberally in my tea, coffee, bowl of canned mixed fruit, cream of mushroom or tomato soup, and often poured it over my breakfast bowl of bran flakes.

Mother also managed to somehow beat the canned evaporated milk into a whipped cream–like dessert topping to be dolloped onto slices of pie or over fruit dessert, the fruit, of course, always from cans; we rarely saw fresh. From whom she learned the art of whipping canned milk is, of course, a mystery. But I must say, she belonged to a typical 1950s housebound, telephone-connected group of equally housebound ladies in town, who stayed home, as did most 1950s housewives, and in idle minutes of conversation, passed on and shared ideas, secrets, recipes, gossip, suggestions, and complaints. Of these, complaints reigned supreme and were frequently well-grounded.

Many housewives residing in the south would have no idea how these northern girls managed to juggle the oddities of a northern wife's life challenges. As I have alluded to, the most common complaints coming down the telephone lines were complaints about the high cost of living. And the villain, the excuse, always boiled down to the cost of northern transportation. It seemed that everything sold was more expensive because they were told of the added expense of transportation. Vegetables, bags of sugar and flour, milk, fruit, canned goods, soap, and soup—you name it—all cost more, with one notable exception. And this exception angered the old man because, you see, this exception was not essential and would doom any politician who argued against it. I am talking about alcohol. Believe it or not, any product sold in the government-owned liquor store, or beer sold by either of the two hotels, was sold at the same price found in any other community in the province. The expense of transportation was, and probably still is, subsidized. Not so for fresh fruit. Not so for cabbages or potatoes. And most definitely not so for milk. This was good news for the casual drinker and those who considered drinking to be a competition, boasting they could out-consume whomever and still be able to drive. But this was bad news for us kids who, to grow up strong and healthy, needed a balanced diet. In fact, it was like Alice looking through the looking glass as the Mad Hatter ran around shouting nonsense, a land where the ridiculous and sensible were reversed and considered as normal. No wonder people in town drank, some all too often to excess. Alcohol was a cheap and convenient way to escape life's sharp edges. Yes, it was the kind of town where some might say that the way to begin the day is by pouring beer, rather than milk, into the bowl of cornflakes at breakfast.

VENUS IN BLUE JEANS

The first of my life's loves was an American girl, who purred with a captivating southern drawl. She was the child of an American serviceman, part of a family that, like many others, was posted to Churchill and then, after two years, as predictable as the thaw in spring, was gone with the snow. The mobility of military families meant that, like nature in that subarctic community, the life span of a young love burned brilliant in the heat of a moment of time and then, in a blink of an eye and an ache in the heart, was gone.

School always commenced on the Tuesday following Labour Day, and by the time Hallowe'en rolled around—because of the early arrival of winter winds, snow, and ice—seasonal activities were in full swing. Along with giving a wide berth to any roaming hungry polar bears, my friends and I skated, played pool and hockey, and curled. For the uninitiated, curling is a game where each team is expected to slide eight 40-pound lumps of Scottish granite, called a "stone" or a "rock," with a degree of accuracy, down a 150-foot-long sheet of pebbled ice to a target made up of three concentric circles, oddly called "the house." I was a confirmed curler, participating in two leagues—the Armed Forces interservice league and the high school league, the latter of which was held every Thursday right after school was dismissed. The rules were simple for the high school curlers: two boys and two girls played any one of the four positions (lead, second, third, or skip), and the game lasted only eight ends instead of the usual ten. Because of my great wealth of experience and seniority (I was sixteen after all), I usually skipped my team. One year, I discovered that an American girl was assigned to my team. She was a year younger than me, and although this was her family's second and final year in Churchill, this was her first attempt at curling. Considering this fact carefully, I asked if she felt comfortable playing lead, the very first team member to throw two stones at the start of each end down the 150 feet of pebbled ice. I did this for two reasons. First, she could, amid the noise of the rumble of other rocks curling and colliding on neighbouring sheets of ice, hopefully place her rocks near, or perhaps in, the house. And second, as her rock curled its way toward me, she could help me to "sweep" her rock to where I hoped it would lie. But I knew it wouldn't arrive. She was, and there is no nice way to put this, hopeless. Most of her rocks did not travel as far as, let alone over, the hog line, where a rock remained "in play," so were shoved with the heel of a shoe out of play, usually to the cry of "Nice try!" from me. And she was less than helpful with her broom when trying to sweep. But give her her due, she certainly tried, vigorously whipping the straw bristles of her broom around a moving rock, usually to no avail. Sometimes, in exasperation, she would suddenly stop sweeping, as she knew the rock had absolutely no future in the game, and then turn and smile at me, shrugging her shoulders as if to say that she at least knew when to quit a losing effort, despite my plaintiff cry of "Sweep harder! Sweep!", from time to time, she would hit a moving rock while she was whipping her broom around, automatically taking a rock or two out of play. And on cue, once again, came that smile and shrug. I began to wonder if her hitting a rock was by design or accident. Or, and this could happen to anyone, she would find her runners slipping away from where her feet wanted to be and fall on her backside, which then often resulted in her accidentally moving a rock or two out of play. And on cue, once again, came that smile and shrug.

I began to wonder, because she was so desperately bad at curling, why she arrived every week on time and attempted to play a game she was obviously not good at and, as a Confederate-born American, would never be good at—and always, always with that smile. But she was persistent and, unfortunately, did not improve with time. Candidly, she was a perfectly horrid curler wrapped in a perfectly beguiling shrug and smile. And, my goodness, she was beautiful. At least I thought so. And this girl, this American girl, was Donna, a girl I honestly believed to be out of my league. Then one day, quite unexpectedly, passing through the swirls of ethers, one of Donna's girlfriends forwarded a carefully crafted cryptic message to a friend of mine that said (and I may add that here it gets confusing) one of her friends wanted to perhaps be more than friends with me. And by the way, I could have created a successful TV sitcom about friends out of this concept and, in the process, could have made millions. But I didn't, of course.

When it comes to deciphering women, I was, and probably still am, not the sharpest pencil in the pencil box. In fact, cryptic messages usually fly over the heads of most guys and are thrust directly into outer space. Right now, I'd wager that there are probably millions of cryptic messages buzzing aimlessly around the International Space Station, looking hopefully through the windows, looking for a place to land. Let's face it, men are wired differently. Like dogs, we live in a basic black-and-white world, and if we are fed and watered, our needs met, and our tummies scratched occasionally, we are happy. So, it never occurred to me that such a lovely Georgia peach pie sort of girl would want to date me. It was, in my mind, highly improbable. For starters, she came from a different world than me. Her father was an officer in the United States Air Force; mine, a tradesman. My family was firmly rooted in the lore of the English working-class; was left wing, pro-union, largely indifferent to the establishment and the Crown and established religion; rarely drank anything stronger than tea; never owned a house; and ate simply. Hers, on the other hand, I believed was doubtlessly right wing, very conservative, myopically patriotic, most certainly religious in a Southern Baptist sort of way and owned not just a house but probably a family plantation too. They were, in my mind, the kind of people who enjoyed consuming bottles of French wine and fine brandy and ate filet. And I picked the word "filet" because I knew it was a fancy French word for fancy cuts of meat enjoyed by fancy rich people. And as if to plant the flag on the top of Everest, the ultimate of mountains, I faced the ultimate of challenges. Donna was an American, a citizen of a pesky nation I had spent much of my time and effort making fun of. In my mind, I could almost hear God laughing in his bed at the joke he had played on me, as St. Peter, also laughing, brought God his morning cup of coffee, boiled eggs, and toast.

So, it was do or die, and I had only the intent of "doing." I was nervous and apprehensive, but I made the decision to climb the divide that lay between us, to reach the top and then fall over the side, pick myself up, brush the dust off uncertainly, and stand face-to-beautiful-face with her. Then I would screw up my courage, push down my fears, and ask her if she would like to go to the pictures with me. In my head, I had rehearsed a speech.

"I'll pick you up at six for the six-thirty movie and take you to the pictures. I promise, I'll be a complete gentleman and be absolutely enthralled just to be with you. I promise. Honest. Please come to the pictures with me."

At least, that was how I planned it, imagined it. Instead, all I could manage was to grunt, "Like to go to the pictures?"

I looked down and then slowly lifted my head and stared into her eyes. She smiled that smile. I was smitten, jelly kneed.

"Yes, I would," she replied, looking straight at me. Her smile was pure Georgia sunshine.

What? I was stunned. What did she say? Did she say yes? Really? REALLY? She said yes? Of all the words in all the languages, "yes" can be the sweetest.

All was then arranged. I would pick her up at her house at 6:00 p.m. on Friday. And I would be brushed, washed, and polished for the date. Why, I would wear for the occasion a new white T-shirt under a smart almost-new sweater, a pair of blue jeans with a rolled-up and stylish three-inch cuff, and (purchased from the Eaton's catalogue, of course) a brand-new pair of tan-coloured suede shoes, shoes that always included in the box a square sponge with a black gritted surface on one side to remove stubborn stains or marks. And to top off the ensemble, I'd wear my surplus US Air Force parka, purchased by my mother from the United Army and Navy Surplus store in Winnipeg.

Now, I want to make a fact abundantly clear again: Donna's father was an officer in what was and still is the world's most powerful air force. He attended the Officers' Mess, where I imagined all sorts of snooty events were held and where, for a while, my mother worked as a waitress, possibly at his beck and call. He and his family were from a stratosphere where neither I nor my parents were from, nor comfortable in. She was, I believed, most certainly from Venus, both the gleaming evening and morning stars rolled into one. And then there was me, a gawky, working-class sixteen-year-old with, as if to prove my manhood, a soft pack of twenty cigarettes shoved up the left sleeve of my T-shirt. I secretly saw myself, as in the movies, like Humphrey Bogart, who often lit two cigarettes, one for him and the other for her.

On Friday, I boarded the 5:30 p.m. bus in the town square as it waited for passengers next to the flagpole with the weather-worn Red Ensign fluttering from atop, the circle of white and painted stones around the flagpole, and the two ancient cannons that stood stoically on guard. And by 6:00 p.m., there I was, knocking nervously on Donna's front door. Then BOOM! The spell broke, as in a Disney movie, and the wicked stepmother, in the form of a United States Air Force officer and the American father of a girl I really liked, opened the door. I shrank back instinctively. He was still in his uniform and more than intimidating for a sixteen-year-old boy. He said nothing. He didn't have to. There were no words I knew that would convey the message his eyes spoke. The proverbial ball was obviously in play, in my part of the court. What to say? How to say it?

"Hello." My mouth was spitless, dry with fear. My voice croaked, and I attempted a smile that I'm sure looked like a grimace on a gargoyle. "Is Donna home?"

He looked at me. "Young man."

His voice sounded just like Hollywood God in the movies. It was God speaking with an American accent. I was dumbstruck.

"Young man. I expect you to have my daughter home by ten. Do you understand?" He did not smile. I nodded, dumbstruck, terrified of God in a USAF uniform.

In retrospect, with the experience of a life passed like water under a bridge, I realize that standing before me was the worried father of a beautiful daughter who believed that every boy who suddenly showed up for a date was the enemy, whose only interest, he was convinced, was to deflower his little girl. And at that moment, I must have reminded him of his youthful days, those youthful, carefree days.

"Yes sir," I croaked.

The lack of spit in my mouth made talking difficult. I was scared of him. He was intimidating. He was a man who obeyed and followed orders from his superiors and a man who gave orders to and expected obedience from me. I was his subordinate; I was to obey.

"Ten then. No later. Do you understand?" He stared right through me, the last three words fired like bullets from a gun.

"Yes sir."

"Ten. No later," he repeated. The stare continued. And then, with that, he reluctantly stood aside and released Venus, a vision of beauty, a fifteen-year-old goddess in Grade 10. I melted. The captain glared.

Then the goddess spoke. "See you later, Dad."

She kissed his cheek; his face softened, almost glowed. He obviously adored his daughter; you could see it. But he hated me. You could see that too.

The following hours flew by. We went to the pictures, where, I might add, I held her hand. And then, after the movie concluded, we spent a glorious two hours in the canteen upstairs from the theatre. We sat at the counter near the jukebox, and we laughed when she talked of her attempts to curl. She smiled that smile and told me that she had not shown up week after week because she liked curling.

"Do you think—actually think—I like blisters on my hands from sweeping?" she asked.

At first this confession didn't register, but then came the dawn. She liked *me*, not curling. She really liked me. Then I took her home. Fifteen minutes late. And just as Cinderella's golden coach had turned into a pumpkin at midnight, my wicked stepmother in the form of a US Air Force captain was there. Waiting. Waiting just for me. He was furious and allowed himself permission to give me the worst tongue-lashing anybody, including my old man, who was pretty good at a tongue-lashing, could hand out. It was beyond a doubt my very worst tongue-lashing ever!

The *Reader's Digest* condensed version of this tongue-lashing could be summed up in these five statements:

1) Can you tell me the time, young man?

2) Can you not respect a father's wishes, young man?

3) Do you ever defy your father, young man?

4) Who do you think you are, young man?

   and

5) I'll be darned if Donna ever goes out with you again, young man.

The last statement was the clincher. The definitive statement. The *coup de grâce*. What he was really saying—and this message did not, like most, fly over my head and into space—what he was really saying and certainly meant was, "Don't you ever darken my door again. Don't bother with my little girl. Or I will most certainly kill you, young man."

Donna cried. I could hear her in the hallway behind the door. I felt awful and then, miserably, left to catch the last bus home. My perfect evening with a perfect girl had become a perfect symphony of horrors. And why? All for fifteen crappy minutes. I was the epitome of the perfect idiot.

I didn't tell Dad what had happened. At the time, I believed he wouldn't understand. I now know I was wrong. But I told Mum. She told me not to worry; I was young and there were lots of fish in the sea. But at the time, only one girl meant anything to me. I was miserable.

Monday came. Donna was at school, and I avoided her and said nothing. Then came Tuesday, Wednesday, and Thursday, and again I avoided her and said nothing. Truth be told, I didn't have a clue what to say, so avoidance was my solution. And to add to the situation, I was terrified of her father. As usual, Thursday high school curling was in full swing after school, and, incredibly, Donna showed up with her broom and smile, ready to play. I could not believe my eyes. And make no mistake. I was happy to see her. Believe me. And again, she pretended to curl, fell on her bum on the ice again, and got up with that grin. And at the end of the game, she came up to me, face to face, eye to eye.

"Go on," she said.

She stared at me. She dared me.

"Ask me out again. Ask me."

So, I did. No shit! I did and she said, "Yes." She said yes! The world was technicolour again. She told me to pick her up at home the next day at 6:00 p.m., and I was both entranced and terrified. I mean, she was sweet, but her old man, on orders, killed for a living, something like a member of a legal mafia. However, the vision of Venus before me was enough to overcome the fact that her dad was a really, really, scary part of the military mob. It was now time for me to reciprocate and screw up my courage.

The next evening, filled with dread almost like one condemned to the gallows, I made my way by bus and then foot to her house, stared for what seemed an eternity in hell at her front door, and then, as if in anticipation of the worst, hesitantly knocked. I was terrified. Could her father, with a weapon of some sort, be waiting behind the door, waiting to bludgeon me to a pulp or even kill me? Instead, the door opened, and an attractive, pleasant lady—who I surmised to be Donna's mother and who I found also possessed the same beguiling Georgia peach pie accent—was standing there. And

Donna stood smiling behind her. But the captain could not be seen. The mother spoke.

"Harold," she paused. "Harold, I do believe y'all have something to say to this young man."

Harold came down the stairs and stood next to his wife. He seemed somehow defeated, deflated, browbeaten. Incredibly, he then apologized. Yes. I said he apologized. I was not to be beaten to death after all. I perked up. Then, like Saul on the road to Damascus, I was instantly struck by a simple, never-forgotten fact of life. The women in this household had somehow cornered Harold, a captain in the United States Air Force, into giving up. It was then I felt acutely aware of the power of a greater being, and that greater being was distinctly female. I learned that evening that no matter who you think you are, a man crosses a woman at his own peril. This was the best lesson of all the lessons I learned anywhere. Ever!

"I am sorry, young man."

The words sounded as if they were being pulled out painfully by a hook and line, but he said them. He apparently didn't know or refused to say my name.

"But I must tell you," He added, as if to cement his authority at home, "I must tell you that when I ask you to bring Donna home at a certain hour, please try to do so."

The words "please" and "try," I now realize, were not words usually uttered by a man used to direct authority. They were words uttered by someone desperate, who faced certain defeat on the home front, at the foot of the females in his house if he failed to capitulate. He then smiled wanly and stuck out his hand to me, as if in friendship, with some degree of hesitation. I took it. I then shook the hand of a captain in the United States Air Force. At that moment, I felt something slip from his palm to mine. Although I was unaware of what it was, I held onto it with my thumb and palm.

He then turned quickly. His face softened at the sight of Donna. This moment was to be, I now believe, one of many inner struggles he would have reconciled himself to, was the string of boys his daughter would certainly bring home for his grudging approval. I am positive none would meet his approval measuring stick.

"See y'all at ten, Honey. And phone if you have to."

He glanced sideways at me. This was my reminder too. She would, I determined, be home by ten. And that something he slipped into my palm? Turned out to be a five-dollar bill. Did she know? She never mentioned it, so I think not. I prefer to believe that it was a symbolic agreement between a father and a boyfriend who made peace with each other. He got what he wanted, Donna home by ten and restoration of his mastery at home, and I got to date Donna within his rules of conduct.

We dated for five or six months. Then, like the passing of the seasons, her family left for places and bases, perhaps exotic, perhaps not, elsewhere around the world. I have wondered where she finally landed. I just lost touch and wish her well, my first in a succession of Venuses that lasted until the summer of 1969 when I married the reigning Queen of Venus, the last of my life's loves.

I'LL HAVE MINE ON THE
ROCKS, PLEASE

The rocks that ring the shores of Hudson Bay are a natural bookmark, marking that genesis moment billions of years ago when the earth was in the throes of creation. These rocks are so old, there are no other rocks on the surface of the planet older than they are. Born of heat and fire, assaulted by the glacial movement of ice and the passing of time, these shoreline rocks resemble a great grey dam holding back the frigid waters of Hudson Bay in the summer and the craggy formations of ice in the winter that, with the June breakup, heave, crack, rise, and fall with the constant movement and swell of the tides beneath, responding to the gravitational pull of the moon. These rocks have weathered into voluptuous, almost-feminine swells and curves, artfully decorated by nature's makeup with red and orange and green splashes of lichens painted artfully onto their surfaces. On warm, sunny days, lukewarm pools of saltwater are found in the shallow depressions with the retreat of the tide and, on those rare warm, sunny days, become paddling pools for local kids who, in the company of watchful mothers, splash and enjoy an equally rare seaside beach outing.

And we, also on one of those rare warm, sunny days, with vigour and the cocky "I'm invincible" attitude of youth, would try swimming in the near-freezing waters of the Bay. And no matter the air temperature, the waters of the bay remained, stubbornly, just a few degrees above freezing. Lemming-like, we'd migrate to the shore, find a convenient spot that caught the sun yet was sheltered from the breeze that inevitably blew inland, drape out the towels, and then, when the moment was deemed appropriate, remove our jeans, T-shirts, and socks and, with a herd instinct, run in.

The stay in the water was usually brief. The adventurous tried swimming; the hesitant simply stood, knee deep. Then when our bodies were numb, we'd run back to the shelter and towels and sit, shivering in the breeze with the towels draped around our shoulders and necks.

To a botanist, and luckily for the plants I certainly do not consider myself a botanist, these rocks that appear hostile to life attest to the fact that plant life can, in fact, exist among them. I have already mentioned the lichens that survive and appear to thrive on the surface of the rock they choose to cling to, forming red, orange, and green swirls and patterns and are indifferent to the temperature, whether it is +30°C or –30°C.

And apparently, there are dozens of other varieties of dwarf plants, all of which I was oblivious to, that live and then die in that incredibly short summer season. These plants live, I have been informed, in a microclimate found only centimetres from the ground, hugging a tiny envelope of warm air close to the surface.

I have seen fully mature coniferous trees that elect to grow horizontally, hugging the ground rather than growing vertically, as most sensible trees seem to prefer. How the plants and trees and nature get together to figure this out is beyond me, but I have long learned that nature is adaptable and creative and is certainly not to be fooled with. And the trees that do choose the vertical rather than the horizontal also allow one to see how nature chooses to work. The flat, horizontal tree takes full advantage of the warmth of the ground-hugging microclimate in summer and is covered with a layer of insulating snow in winter, whereas the vertical tree, although fully grown, is short, spindly, and virtually branchless on the side facing the prevailing wind. The height, girth, and lack of branches are all ways nature enabled the tree to survive in a climate dominated by bitter winter winds blowing off the Bay and cold temperatures that can only be described as "extreme."

In my youthdom, when I was a typical yobbish lout, I was simply not aware of—not in the least interested in—this miracle of nature. Alas, I was only interested in two things:

Girls. That part of nature did interest me. A lot. And that was obvious, although I was too tongue-tied and awkward to be anything that even slightly resembled a Romeo.

Anything else that caught my fickle fancy for the moment. These interests were flighty and flitted in my brain like a cage full of birds, until one landed and, for that briefest of moments, captivated my attention.

So it was that the beluga whales caught my attention. They were hard to ignore, swam the Bay and Churchill River estuary in impressive numbers, often swimming perilously close to shore.

I saw mothers, herding their kids off to school. I saw them cut the surface of the water in numbers, blowing, and sucking in the air. And I saw them chased, corralled, and killed by hunters in canoes powered by outboards that could outrun and confuse their prey.

At the time, the beluga was legally hunted, and the resulting trophy towed to a processing plant located on the Churchill River flats. The plant had weather worn letters *ADANAC* printed on the side facing town, and I am sure that disgusting things were done to the whales in there. The belugas were, to use the term, "rendered," as they entered one end of the plant as a complete animal and emerged at the other end as—well to be honest—I don't know or want to think about it. And as for the stink! It was awful. Today, no tourist would visit if the plant were still in operation. The smell hovered over the town like a great grey cloud, raining dark odours, even though the sun shone brightly.

Thus, belugas were born, lived, and died in the Hudson Bay waters, following the natural inevitable cycle of life. And occasionally, a beluga that had completed its life cycle would be inevitably blown by the winds and carried by the tides and currents and washed ashore. Then nature would take over and begin the process of decomposition, and an unfortunate side effect of decomposition was the natural production of an overpoweringly evil olfactory punch in the nose.

To us, the smell was revolting, but to a chorus of birds and gangs of four-legged meat eaters, it was a bonanza, a supermarket of goodies, with banners carried on the winds advertising that something very ripe and tasty was waiting down on the beach. Also following the siren call of the breezes, among the zoo of carrion scavengers, came the dogs. Our dogs. Domesticated dogs of every breed who ate in our kitchens and snoozed on our couches, came to rejoice at the table and quarrel over the banquet, a table laid out by Mother Nature herself.

And our dog, Tippie, was no exception. Despite being well fed at home, needing no more nutrition than we provided, he too followed his nose, the winds leading him to the beluga banquet. He loved dead belugas. He loved the smell of dead belugas. And he followed his nose to rummage in the remains of dead belugas. And the need to become singularly perfumed with the stink of dead belugas proved even stronger than his fear of the old man, a person whom I, at least, feared almost as much as anyone feared God, who had the power to make it rain for forty days and forty nights and drown everybody except Noah and his clan. After feasting and rollicking at the beach-party table, Tippie would appear at our back door, tail wagging, in oblivious ignorance of what would happen next.

Suddenly, the excitement of being home gave way to the horror of my old man grabbing his collar and dragging him out behind the house and down to the rocks. I followed, armed with a bottle of my Mother's favourite dish detergent in hand. You know the dish detergent brand—the kind that Madison Avenue claimed could wash 1,000 dishes and, in the process, was so kind to your hands that it made them look years younger. Dad was not in the least interested in these claims, but he was interested in neutralizing the dog's brain-stunning odour of decomposition. Dad was not a cruel man. In a way, he loved that old dog, but he was practical. If a cleansing did not happen, the dog was to be relegated to a sentence of solitary confinement, tied up to a post near our back door, a fate that neither I nor Dad nor, I am sure, Tippie wanted. Unfortunately for Tippie, when the old man arrived at his well-chosen destination, a rock high enough so that he did not get his feet wet from the swelling tide, yet within easy reach of the water, and high enough so that Tippie could find depth and swim ashore, the dreadful deed began. In went Tippie, legs frantically swimming even before he hit the water. Down scrambled the old man to retrieve the poor animal as he struggled in, off came the top of the detergent bottle, and Tippie was well and truly washed. I have no idea if the soap was "Summer Breeze," "Green Apple," or "Lemony Lemon." He was bathed and washed and then, looking somewhat like a squirming bag of black cotton, was unceremoniously cast back into the freezing cold water. How he survived is beyond me, and a couple of dunkings later, he was more or less deodorized and allowed to slink home. And strange to tell, he was thereafter reluctant to come to Dad when

Dad called for weeks on end. The old saying "You can't teach an old dog new tricks" did not exactly ring true here, as Tippie did learn that seeing a man holding a bottle of liquid detergent ended badly—for the dog. But he never learned that the siren call of a dead beluga should be ignored.

At this juncture in my rambles through my youth, I must discuss the "to-ings" and "fro-ings" of my friends and me in our little home away from home located in Norm's backyard. It was simply called "the shack." We had taken over a small, shed-like building that in an earlier life had been the playhouse for his younger sister, Beth, who had since abandoned it for boys. It was a simple building with a peaked roof, a front door, and a side window. Its foundation was of concrete blocks with two-by-four beams and a plywood floor. It was very basic but, to the eyes of a fifteen-year-old, magnificent.

We built in bunks from scrounged wood and then furnished it with bits and bobs from various sources. We ran an electrical cord from Norm's house to the shack for unlimited free power and used a light source liberated from Dad's workshop, with a convenient hook on the bulb's shield to attach to handy nails banged in for the purpose. We also had an ancient tube-filled radio that, when attached to Norman's dad's free power source, could, in the evening, receive Winnipeg's CKY Radio 58, the home of "Manitoba's Friendly Giant," after the radio tubes warmed up for a minute or two, of course.

It was in the shack we attempted to make chemical equations come to life from chemicals purloined from a school with very loose rules regarding student proximity to chemicals, and equipment that was liberated from the lab in the folds of our parkas. Luckily, in the process of playing with these chemicals, we neither burned down the building nor set fire to ourselves.

We would, on a Saturday evening, bribe some cooperative person over the age of twenty-one to purchase for us a dozen beers. Finding someone to purchase our beer was rarely a problem, despite the constant heroic attempts of the local constabulary to end this illicit trade in alcohol.

Thus, in those golden days of a subarctic summer, with daylight lasting for twenty hours and twilight a mere four hours, we would sit in our beloved shack, tell tall stories, and boast of our mostly imaginary sexual conquests. We would drink our beer, turn on the radio to Winnipeg's CKY Radio 58, and listen to the deejay allotted the night shift and to the pop tunes of the time. Funny thing, as I sit in my seventh decade and keep myself busy for fear of rusting, I still listen to those tunes and am transported back to those times. It all seems like yesterday.

Life was indeed good. We had a lifetime ahead of us and beers in our hands. We sat, looking northwest, as the sun sank slowly and began its drop below the horizon. Then, with the sun gone, the sky took on a purple, half-light hue.

With our last bottle of beer finished, and 95 percent of Churchill's population safely tucked in their beds, we turned off the radio, closed the door to the shack, and headed for the rocks behind the Roman Catholic church. Once on the rocks, we wandered, looking for a comfortable pew that nature had carved, and settled down to watch the sun begin its rise, marking a new day.

It is now necessary for me to say that never in my life have I been so fortunate as to experience this simple act of nature. The rising of the sun. A subarctic dawn. A new day. To have watched the sun rising as it did so many years ago, I am not surprised that the glory of a new day dawning over such a great expanse of sky and water made such an impression on the mind of a fifteen-year-old blank canvas waiting to be painted. No wonder the sun was at the centre of the Pantheon of gods and worshipped by our ancestors. And to think, most of us choose to miss the dawn for sleep. Then, at least, a fifteen-year-old and his friends knew better and were content to let the old-timers take their eight-hour snooze and leave the world, albeit temporarily, to us.

The rocks were the natural playground for numerous kids on long warm, sunny days. As lanky teenagers, we would jump from one rock to another, sometimes jumping crevices a couple of metres deep. Sometimes, somebody would slip and fall while jumping from one ledge to another, calling for a trip to the doctor, usually for no more than bloody scrapes. There were times when somebody fractured a bone, but it was indeed well worth it. It was absolutely splendid. How could life get any better than this?

For me, the answer was found on a warm June evening, when I should have been studying for my final Grade 11 math exam. On the pretext of studying at Wayne's, we abandoned our books and walked the beach between the rocks and water. It was a perfect evening. Still. Sunny. Calm. And in the silence of the evening, we watched a great mass of floating ice turn over, filling the air with a sound that roared out its power. Then a great wash of water circled away from the ice as it broke into yet smaller pieces. A curious seal, perhaps wondering what all the fuss was about, poked its head above the water and swirled in circles the way seals do. Then as suddenly as it appeared, it was gone.

And yes, I passed that exam, and others, because I was expected to—albeit by the skin of my teeth. But at the time, to be quite honest, I was quite content sitting on the rocks, feeling the breeze blow off the Bay, and listening to the music of the ice chiming as it moved and jostled with the tide and breeze against other floating chunks. I was, I knew, the luckiest of boys. I was, I was positive, in God's living room, and privileged to be there, sitting with Him.

SATURDAY NIGHT AT THE MOVIES

To be perfectly honest, I rarely attended the movies on a Saturday night. Friday night was movie night. Saturday was reserved for other activities. If I had been on a rare date with a real girl on Friday—and all had gone well on that date—then Saturday evening was often spoken for, if she was not otherwise engaged in babysitting, or some other excuse dreamed up by a father who harboured a fierce antipathy toward teenaged boys in general, and me in particular. But as dates were few and far between—and suspicious fathers numerous—we did the next best thing and searched for someone, anyone over twenty-one, who would be open to a financial bribe in exchange for his purchasing for us a case of beer, or a bottle of rye, rum, or vodka. We were not connoisseurs and were rarely fussy; we had yet to develop a taste for blended Scotch whisky.

But looking back through the prism of time, I know that Friday was the day we all looked forward to. As soon as the 4:00 p.m. school bell rang out its call to freedom, signalling the end of the week and the commencement of two days off, we knew we were footloose and fancy free. Friday was indeed the very best day of the whole week, a day to be relished and savoured, unless, of course, it was Good Friday. Good Friday was like a Sunday but a hundred times worse. It was an entire day with absolutely nothing to do, a day spent at home, with everything I liked—the movie house, bowling alley, pool hall—closed, but not the evangelical church located next door. Fascinated, I would watch the Good Friday faithful waving their arms with, occasionally, one member standing with arms raised, apparently shouting heavenly inspired messages toward the ceiling.

Yes, even then at a tender age, I was fast becoming a religious skeptic, a skepticism I had developed several years prior when I discovered that Santa

Claus, a being I had blindly believed in because I was told he was real, was really a hoax foisted upon me and countless other children by parents and grandparents and some of Canada's largest department stores and a large soft drink manufacturer—a hoax perpetuated on trusting children as a foil to "Be good or else . . ." and to "Go to bed now or you-know-who won't be coming down the chimney," a chimney and fireplace that, in our house, didn't exist anyway, although I really believed that one would magically appear, just for Santa, on Christmas Eve because I was told it would appear.

Our house, a simple, tiny frame structure with faux-brick nailed-on siding, stood a stone's throw behind the local movie theatre and the local pool hall and bowling alley. The pool hall was a place frowned upon by the old man, who forbade me to patronize it. In his mind, it was a den of iniquity. To my mind, it was the forbidden fruit, always beckoning, tantalizingly calling, impossible to resist. Therefore, after school, upon departing the bus in the town square, I—in defiance—patronized the establishment. And there, I learned to smoke, hung out with the permanent resident ne'er-do-wells who held up the walls, and learned the finer points of pool, although I never did really master the art to be considered a threat to the other pool players.

The movie theatre in Fort Churchill that my friends and I attended, without fail, every Friday evening. was the Garrison Theatre. This was just a twenty-minute bus ride down the highway. We boarded the local hourly bus parked in the town square, still parked next to the flagpole with the same time-worn, tatty Canadian Red Ensign fluttering in the breeze and the two ancient cannons guarding the flagpole and the flag.

Paying the driver, we'd head for the back seats, excited in anticipation of the bright lights and the pretty girls of Fort Churchill. We were noisy, shoving each other and laughing, and found that other passengers would give us "the look." Our parents would have been proud, I'm sure, especially when, with a flourish, we lit our cigarettes and blew smoke at each other.

The ride from the townsite to Fort Churchill, which we commonly referred to as "camp," was over a potholed gravel strip we called "the highway." In winter, the bus itself offered little in the way of creature comforts. It was cold, heated primarily by our bodies and the act of breathing. As a result, the windows were coated with a thick layer of opaque ice, making it impossible to see exactly where the bus was in relation to one's destination. As a diversion, we idly pressed a thumb, finger, or palm onto the ice-covered glass, usually in a vain attempt to melt a hole into the ice.

The bus was always crowded on the afternoon trip home from school. It functioned, you see, not only as the school bus but also as a bus open to any other fare-paying passenger who needed a ride. Consequently, we would jam ourselves into the seats, the farther back the better. And the girls, who were terrible flirts anyway and were at least five years ahead of us boys in maturity, although the same age chronologically, would sit on our laps. One pretty girl on whom I had a desperate crush—and she knew it and knew how to play me like a fiddle—would settle onto my lap and stare into my brown eyes with her brown eyes. She was a super flirt, the queen of flirts. And I was smitten with her, although deep down I could see nothing developing from these encounters. And she, apart from my mother and my ever-patient wife, was the only person I ever allowed to call me "Johnny."

But I digress. On a Friday evening, the bus would bounce and bang on worn-out shocks down the highway toward camp. On its way, it would stop in front of HMCS Churchill if a passenger wished to board or get off and then continue on into Camp 20, the local home to a population of Inuit, who would board, always, I recall, smiling and wearing those very characteristically styled Inuit parkas. Every once in a while, a mother, with her baby snuggled in the folds of the parka she wore, would disembark at the hospital to attend the Well Baby Clinic. The mother would, as a matter of course, feed her child. This, although uncomfortable for some, was to be taken as a matter of course by most. Few paid any attention.

After Camp 20, the bus rattled on, heading toward the guardhouse and then the hill that marked the entrance to Fort Churchill. The thing I recall clearly about the guardhouse was that it was often, but not always, manned. And never once in memory did the lonely guard depart the guardhouse, stop traffic, and demand to know the business of the persons trying to enter the base.

Thus, if all went well, and if the bus did not stall on the slope heading toward the base, we would arrive at our destination close to an entrance that led to a corridor that took us past the Men's Mess and the theatre entrance. The Men's Mess had a space across from the doors where the soldiers hung their hats, which they could not wear inside the mess. Many of us boys possessed a donated US Army hat, which we sometimes wore on our expeditions in the bush. So, may I now say to that soldier who donated his hat to me, "I'm sorry."

On past the Men's Mess was the theatre, which showed three movies a week. It was closed on Thursdays. At 6:00 p.m., the doors to the theatre opened, and the crowd waiting in the corridor moved toward the cashier's booth. The cost? Fifteen cents for a student and thirty-five cents for an adult. The snack bar offered a good variety of sweets. Want a Cherry Blossom? My favourites, at ten cents. A box of popcorn? Again, a dime. No butter flavouring, though, and no soft drinks. But there was water in the fountain. The water was never chilled, and sometimes, because the water lines ran through utilidors that also carried hot steam lines, the water could be unpleasantly warm.

The boys always chose seats in the centre of the theatre, one or two rows behind the inevitable gaggle of girls who giggled and whispered to each other as they took sideways glances back. We knew they were talking about us, so, in a manly way, we did the natural things a male of fifteen would do. We showed off. It was the equivalent of the peacock showing his feathers to the pea hen, except in this case, we were the scruffy ones, and the girls had made the effort to look pretty. And in general, they were successful.

Very occasionally, a boy would luck out with a girl, and the pair would migrate to the back seats of the theatre. But for most of us, for most of the time, this was only wishful thinking. Yes, the movie theatre was a petri dish of male and female hormones, all swimming around and very occasionally bumping into each other. But the reality was that little bumping actually occurred. Oh, we acted tough and bragged about girls and conquests, but it was all just imaginative smoke and mirrors and lies. Truthfully, we all were beginning the human journey into adulthood that is always preceded by those tumultuous and often horrible adolescent years.

Again, looking back, many of us survived the angst of those teenage years and managed to find good partners with whom to share our lives. A few did not. But that is the way luck and chance work—pure Darwinism at work, I suppose. And for me, it all started with an ancient yellow bus taking me to and from school on weekdays or to movies on Friday evenings. School gave me the ticket to get an education and pursue a reasonable living. The movies, on the other hand, introduced me to the tinsel world of Hollywood, the make-believe cooked up by the studios of Warner Brothers, MGM, and RKO—Doris Day comedies and John Wayne westerns and war stories of an American world showcasing American values and American glitter. And it was also on the bus, at school, or at the movies where I started the quest for the holy grail, trying to solve the puzzle that is the female of the species. And may I also say years and years later, I have not been fully successful in that quest. The mystery of the female puzzle continues, compounded now by the arrival of my three grandchildren. All girls. Each an enigma.

I LOVE, I LOVE, I LOVE
MY CALENDAR GIRLS

For many of the inhabitants of this planet we call home, we mark the commencement of the year, where we were taught it begins, on January 1, and its conclusion twelve months later on December 31. And in between these dates, in equal quarters, we mark the four seasons. So enchanted was Vivaldi that he felt compelled to compose, with pen strokes of musical genius, a celebration of the four seasons. And I have no quarrel with Vivaldi. Who am I to quarrel with a musical genius? My dispute has little to do with the characteristic beauty of the four seasons or their sequence. After all, spring must surely follow winter. It is a given, spelled out by the celestial positioning of the earth and the sun, and thank goodness we have yet to figure out a way to disturb this arrangement. Rather, my personal dispute is with the calendar itself, where we have proclaimed the new year to begin and the old year to simply fade away. And in my mind, the new year never, ever begins with the traditional January 1st.

At this juncture, I can sense the ire of all the Scots around the world, and there are lots of them, who have made New Year's Eve celebrations the epicentre of Scottish national pride. Why Scotland so values New Year's Eve celebrations is beyond me. It is the only nation I know of that adheres to a two-day holiday: one to presumably celebrate and the other to recover. And, for the cherry on the cake, the *pièce de résistance*, the Scots have even taken to exporting to the western world Robbie Burns's incomprehensible "Auld Lang Syne," a song with words that few (and this includes many Scots) actually comprehend. Thus, on New Year's Eve, like trained parrots, at midnight, we attempt to sing with words we don't understand. Strange indeed!

Now let's get down to brass tacks. If I do not agree with the millions of printed January 1st to December 31st calendars, often offered free by banks and realtors, insurance companies, and, last but not least, tool manufacturers (reminding us on a day-to-day basis of their products that are often inexplicably in the hands of scantily clad, sexy, curvaceous young women draped over the seat of a Harley), then what do I adhere to? Let's remember, I was a student in schools and university for a grand total of seventeen years and then a professional educator for over three decades. Subsequently, for me, my calendar year always and forever would commence, not on January 1st but on the Tuesday after Labour Day. This was the day the academic year would begin, in both the public school system and universities. Consequently, this was when my new year began. It then continued through the months, passing Thanksgiving, Hallowe'en, Remembrance Day, Christmas Eve, Christmas Day, Boxing Day, New Year's Eve and New Year's Day, Pancake Tuesday, Good Friday, and Easter Sunday, on through the cold winds of March and April showers and Queen Victoria's birthday, and my birthday, at the end of May. And then the magic commenced with July 1st—Canada Day. Summer dawned. Two whole months. Two glorious months. Two sun-drenched months to loaf around; water the flowers; paint doors, walls, and windows frames; go to the cottage by the lake; fish; read; go to the beach and make sure my two boys played safely in the sand or only paddled in shallow water on the beach. July and August. Two months that flew by. Two summer months carved out of the ancient Roman calendar by these two insufferable Roman egos, Julius and his adopted son, Augustus, who, in fits of self-obsession, declared that the very best two months of the year be named in their honour and, in the process, changed a sensible ten-month year into a weird twelve. As a child, and into my awkward, gawky teenaged years, I subconsciously saw those two carefree summer months as empty roads, ready to traverse wherever I chose. I was left to roam freely, digging holes in the backyard, losing my Dinky toys in those holes, and then, upon reaching thirteen, acquiring a real two-wheeled bike, roaming wherever my youthful legs and bike would take me roaming with my friends.

My parents had little inclination nor interest in spending scarce cash on organized summer activities, if indeed any such activity existed. As a matter of fact, there were no lessons period! I was set loose to run free. No swimming classes, no music, no gymnastics, no skating classes, and no dance classes.

Thank God! I just cannot imagine a life co-existing with my chums had I been exiled to dance classes.

Instead, at seven or eight, I dug holes and played with, and lost, my Dinky toys. And later, as I grew older, I got on my bike and rode with my friends, who also had parents of similar inclination and financial restraints as mine. And to put the record straight, most working-class parents in mid-twentieth-century Canada saw the world in a very similar way. Then, abruptly, my life changed. Spun on the proverbial dime. When I turned sixteen in May, and by June I could drive legally, my old man made a decision. He apparently didn't see the summer months as empty shelves to be filled with summer bric-a-brac. No! He insisted, instead, that I aggressively look for and obtain useful employment. The good old boyish years of summer loafing were apparently over. Dead as a dodo bird. Dad, after all, had joined the workforce at the age of fourteen and was a believer in the "Idle hands are the devil's workshop" philosophy. That was an interesting thing about the old man. He reverted to religious quotes whenever it suited his purpose; otherwise, religion was relegated to the back burner, ready to be once again hauled out and used whenever the need called for it.

I was initially reluctant, as working meant rising around 7:00 a.m.; making my way to work; punching in before 8:00 a.m.; being taken to some place to work at things, usually unpleasant; and then after 5:00 p.m., punching out and staggering home. I was usually far too exhausted to wander afield in the evening; physical labour does that to a skinny sixteen-year-old, unfamiliar with the demands of eight hours of work. So, I stayed close to home and went to bed early, which was, I now believe, part of the old man's master plan. He was determined I learn the value of money and appreciate that it didn't grow on trees. I found it didn't. I also suspect he correctly deduced my circle of friends were a bad influence on me and was also determined, in one way or another, to save me from the evil influence of peer pressure. He was absolutely right about peer pressure because the acclamation of my peers proved to be far more powerful than the fear I had for my old man. Hence, despite his titanic efforts, I both secretly smoked roll-your-owns or, in times of prosperity, tailor-made, name brand cigarettes and consumed bottles of illicit beer, the former a habit I thankfully jettisoned years ago. The latter, not so much—although Scotch is now my tipple of choice.

The one wonderful bonus to rising at 7:00 a.m. and working until 5:00 p.m. was that I was paid a mind-boggling $1.65 per hour and, here's the really good part, twenty-five cents extra per hour northern allowance, just for showing up. Money for nothing!

And there you have it. My year consisting of ten academic months, followed by two months of summer. And even as a senior, now retired to a life that consists of a whole week made up entirely of a seven-day weekend, I still habitually follow the pattern of the school year dictating the arrangement of my calendar year. Thus, it was then, when school opened to commence the academic year, on the Tuesday after Labour Day, my fabulous, shiny, brand-new year began—and it still does!

On that magical day school began, my year always commenced with a school assembly, a time when the boys and girls gathered in the gym-cum-auditorium, because it had a stage, to listen to the principal proclaim from that stage words of welcome to the newcomers and words of dire warning aimed primarily at us boys, words hinting at possible exile if we misbehaved. However, the presence of a host of pretty, ponytailed, bobby-socked girls, many newly delivered during the summer months, made the principal's dire proclamation about possible exile well worth ignoring. And believe me, we had become experts at ignoring his missives.

These girls sporting ponytails were the daughters of fathers we boys should have and often did fear. They were the daughters of members of the armed forces, both Canadian and American, who were, by the nature of their business, hired guns who could and would dispatch people on orders. But this fact didn't easily put us off. And, on the sunny side, these girls were living proof, in my mind at least, that a new and hopefully happy new year had just begun.

September brought autumn, which marked the first season of my year and was, in those northerly climes, brief, quickly becoming ominously winter-like. There were no golden and red leaves to rake into piles that kids could jump into, scattering the leaves far and wide; no farmers in conga lines of combines and clouds of wheat chaff, reaping a golden harvest; and no sweet days of late September or early October when, in southern climes, nature would provide, in days growing daily shorter, a contracted burst of summer—a time that was then called, for no apparent reason, "Indian Summer."

But nature, in her predictable way, even that far north, did clearly mark that brief interlude between the long glory days of summer and the brutally short bitter days of winter. There was the breathtaking migration of birds, all mysteriously bound on invisible tracks heading for the warmth of the South, some reaching as far as the equator, all driven by the magnetic pull of migration. Of all the birds departing, I felt sorry for the geese as they took off, as their fate was to be shot at all along their migratory route, many only making it as far as the dinner plates of the hunters.

Another hint that it was indeed autumn were the squalls of rain mixed with snow, squalls that came in relentlessly with the winds off Hudson Bay. These squalls would commence in early September and grow in intensity until October, when it snowed exclusively, settling gently in quiet corners, and blowing in the open, creating small drifts. With the snow, colder temperatures, and the beginning of ice formation in the ditches, puddles, lakes, and on the Bay itself, came lumbering the true harbinger of autumn, the polar bear. He would appear and wander around town lured by the easy pickings found in the town dump—waiting, waiting, waiting patiently for the ice to fully form on the Bay so that he could set off on the hunt. These bears presented a problem to the community. Because they were natural predators, and we were slow moving snacks on two legs who could never outrun a hungry, healthy half-ton of bear at full gallop, I was afraid of them. I recall how the prospect of meeting a bear on the road as I ran from the school bus on the highway to my home terrified me. It was not a great distance, but far enough for a bear to make a quick meal of me. I saw enough bears to give them a wide berth, and a female with a cub or two required an even wider berth, as they could be unpredictable and were very protective of their young. In those days, what were seen as "nuisance bears" were usually shot. Today, thank goodness, that practice has been largely abandoned by using more humane methods, which do not end with a polar bear becoming a rug in front of some millionaire's cottage fireplace.

The shift from summer to winter was swift. In fact, it was so swift that within six or seven weeks, we had abandoned into closets our lightweight windbreakers, our summer shoes and runners, our baseball mitts, our bats and balls, and our fishing rods and lures and hauled out skates, curling brooms, hockey sticks and pucks, winter mitts and scarves, toques, heavy winter boots, parkas, and thick woollen sweaters for another winter, a season that would last for six months. Winter would then finally reluctantly end with the traditional broomball season that made a brief but energetic appearance in May, signalling the last gasp of winter, my birthday, and the heralding of a short, but welcomed, spring. But I get ahead of myself. Before that glorious day that saw spring arrive officially with the vernal equinox, we had to find things to do to occupy ourselves during winter's short, cold days and long, colder nights.

We played cards. We learned deuces wild and blackjack, learned cribbage, and tried to comprehend the mysteries of bridge, which was, to be truthful, beyond us. We listened to music on Norm's sister's record player, playing those almost indestructible 45s and more fragile 33s and, whenever possible, tuned in to distant radio stations on a tube-filled 1950s plastic-cased radio that took forever to warm up. On some rare evenings, the radio provided feasts of hits from cities as far away as Chicago or St. Louis, but on other evenings, nothing but the chatter of white noise. Stations came and went, often disappearing into pure static right in the middle of a song that had caught our interest. It was via radio we heard of The Platters, Dion, Carl Perkins, Chet Atkins, Little Richard, Fats Domino, Brenda Lee, Duane Eddy, Johnny Cash, Bobby Vee, Fabian—an entire pantheon of almost exclusively American artists who would be mowed down in the early sixties by the British Invasion, led by The Beatles, The Dave Clark Five, The Rolling Stones, and Gerry and the Pacemakers.

To pass the time, we attempted hypnotism. It didn't work. We burned farts and tried to guess from the colour of flame what elements were contained within the gas as it leaked and flamed around the seam of our jeans. We read the endless stream of magazines (copies of *Playboy* were pored over closely), we read books, and we talked of girls and lied of our imaginary exploits and conquests. We played pool in the local pool hall, where seventeen- or eighteen-year-old ne'er-do-wells leaned against and held up the walls and would make colourful comments about our lack of skill or lineage, while knocking the end of our cues as we attempted a shot. There were hockey games to attend, games which were admission-free and often violent grudge matches. We attended the movies without fail every Friday evening; curled twice a week; listened to Foster Hewitt on the CBC's *Hockey Night in*

Canada, if reception permitted, describing the play-by-play of an NHL game on a Saturday evening; and, when all else failed, completed, often in a shoddy way, our homework, where we pooled our limited resources. Usually, it was a case of the blind leading the blind and arriving, in a more or less democratic way, at a common consensus. We pondered over math problems, tried to balance a chemical equation, or wondered whether or not we would like to live in Elizabeth Bennett's Regency world. We decided not. We memorized and repeated over and over our compulsory dozen or so lines of Shakespeare, lines I can still, with prodding, recite today, but at the time, like parrots in a cage, learning a string of phrases and words that made little sense to us made us more and more certain we hated Shakespeare, which was too bad. The adage "pearls before swine" comes to mind.

Christmas marked the early climax of the winter, especially for kids who spent endless hours rummaging through the "Christmas Wish Catalogue" from Eaton's, looking for the Mount Everest of gifts, marking a list of what they would like to find lying under the artificial tree on the twenty-fifth. We avoided the sensible offerings—the usual suspects like socks, sweaters, and, worst of all, underwear—and concentrated on the other pie-in-the-sky things such as electric guitars (which I couldn't play), radios (which I could play), and, best of all, in a box that didn't come from Eaton's at all, the keys to the family car. Keys that would enable me to impress any fifteen-year-old girl. Keys that I lusted after. But keys that would never, ever happen. A second moon would appear in the heavens first.

December saw the annual outing of our Christmas tree, proudly stating "MADE IN THE USA" on the box. Ours was a typical example of a late 1950s artificial tree with removable boughs that bent or refused to roost permanently in the holes drilled into the green stick that served as a trunk. This tree coyly emerged from its dark home in the attic each December and, after New Year's Day, hid away for the next eleven months. It resembled a five-foot-high Fuller bristle brush with little similarity to the real thing, except it was indeed green and conical in shape.

With the excitement of Christmas over, followed by the New Year's celebrations that meant more to my parents than to me, we settled into the post–New Year's doldrums. One positive sign once the new year established itself was that gradually, tantalizingly slowly, the number of daylight minutes increased, and the nights grew shorter. But the reality was that the daily temperature of January and February stubbornly refused to budge. And, on some days, the wind kicked up its heels and produced a surface blizzard, although above the swirly snow was blue sky with not a cloud producing a single snowflake. On such days, we kept an ear on the tiny blue-and-white plastic-cased radio in the kitchen, tuned in to CHFC Churchill, to hear the announcer declare whether the windchill and the driving snow battering on the walls of the house Dad had rented meant school was cancelled for the day. If so, my bubble of a world ground to a halt, leaving me with little to do but, if desperate, take a resigned stab at my homework.

March is that blissful month that often marks the appearance of Easter chicks and bunnies, and always the vernal equinox, when the sun crosses the equator, and the official start of spring. It is at this point in the season that the growing power of the sun begins to exert itself with an increase in the number of daylight hours and an ability to warm a room through a glass pane despite sub-zero temperatures on the other side of the window. One can almost sense the world beginning to awaken, stretch, and shake off winter and prepare itself for those lengthening days of spring.

By late March and early April, the expanding number of daylight hours together with the subtle rise of the average daytime temperature allowed us boys to be off on a Saturday morning, heading into the bush and making sure we stuck very close to one of the two easily followed routes. The first route was a military trail, cut through the bush for miles, used by tracked Canadian Army machines called "Penguins," built by Bombardier. Consequently, the trail was called the "Penguin Trail." Penguins were noisy and announced their four-and-a-half-ton presence from a considerable distance. They were used in winter only to transport supplies and troops engaged in winter survival training exercises, one of the reasons for the existence of Fort Churchill. As the Penguins neared us, we moved and stood, often in knee-deep snow, along the verge of the trail until the machines had passed by in a cacophony of noise and flying chunks of track-laden snow. Once gone, we would struggle back onto the trail and watch the last of the Penguins until it disappeared among the trees.

Our second route was to follow the Canadian National rail line that was thrust north in 1929, completing 500 miles that connected The Pas to the

Port of Churchill. This line was usually quiet, especially in winter when the port was closed and there were only three trains a week. The distance north of The Pas was mile-posted, the number attached to a set of tripod telegraph poles. We used these markers to tell us how far we had roamed and to calculate how far the return distance to town would be. Thus, if the weather looked promising, a half-dozen of us would happily wander out in the morning and return in the evening—a tired, leg-weary group straggling home down the CN tracks. And, to prove our identity as men, we all carried single shot .22s. Why? Hard to say, exactly. But to a fifteen- or sixteen-year-old, there was certainly a sense of manhood epitomized by those guns, a sense of manhood I have long since abandoned.

Spring is aptly named. Spring can best be described as a clockwork mechanism wound tight in winter, looking to release the latent pent-up energy that accumulated during those long, dark days. And, like spring, we too were restless, and as the days saw more daylight, winter reluctantly began to relax its grip, and the sap, including ours, began to rise.

Initially, we would take ourselves a few miles down the track and then push off onto the Penguin Trail. But as the days grew longer, the stay would extend overnight to the weekend. We had to dress for the occasion, in shearling-lined boots, ex-military parkas, and snow pants. A toboggan was loaded with an assortment of .22s and the necessities of a weekend. We even found and claimed what we chose to believe to be an abandoned log cabin. It had homemade bunks and a table, a firebox stove, and windows that were largely intact. We moved in and then used it continuously throughout our high school years. And nobody complained. It was our place in the woods—a place we were responsible for and then left for others to enjoy.

The railway south of Churchill was our highway, and we followed it for miles. If a train came through, as it occasionally would, we had plenty of warning. The sound of an approaching train could be heard for miles, travelling through the clear cold air. And then came the light, even in daytime, shining like a diamond, leading the way for the locomotive as it wound slowly to its destination. We moved off the tracks as the train neared and waited, standing in deep snow as the succession of cars flew by in the flurry of loose snow and the vibration of a succession of wheels rolling on steel. Then we struggled back to the railbed and looked down track to see the last car disappear in a swirling vacuum of white. And then it was gone. Dusting the snow loose from our pants, pockets, and boots, we once again set off down the track.

It is peculiar for me to think of how free we were, and how liberal our parents were, allowing us to disappear in the bush, especially for five or six days over the Easter break. We would set off on Good Friday and reappear on the following Thursday or Friday. By day, we wandered the trails, shooting our .22s, lighting fires, and eating our bread and peanut butter. Doug, with his single-shot bolt-action .22 rifle, shot at and succeeded in killing a rabbit he saw loping for safety over the snow's surface. He then recovered his trophy after wading through knee-deep snow and carried it back to the cabin where he skinned it and roasted it, while we watched, telling him to cook it well or he would die from some strange Australian disease that we'd heard of and were sure the rabbit carried. He ate it. He didn't die.

Spring, hinted at in April, finally shrugged off the weight of winter with longer days and warmer temperatures in May. Parkas that had protected us from the worst of winter were finally relocated back into the closet where they would spend the off-season relaxing before they were cleaned in September and put back into service.

With the passing of May and the dawning of June, the vast, open, prairie-like ice-covered Hudson Bay began the process of breakup. And along with the passing of each day came warmer temperatures and longer daylight hours. All of this, together with the constant movement of the tides, caused the ice to begin to yield its grip, producing jostling, moving ice sheets—some large, some small, some turning top to bottom with the groan and surge of water. Spring also saw the return of the birds, all following the magical migratory routes, ready to nest and to do whatever it is nature drives birds to do in the spring. At the time, we kids had no idea how unique the birds of Churchill were nor how far they migrated. For us kids, they were just birds.

And with spring came broomball. The melting of the ice in the arena signalled the end of the blood sport called hockey, and the brief broomball season began. It was the last organized sport in the arena before the shutdown for the summer.

The broomball season was mercifully short, no longer than three or four weeks. All that was needed was a total team of around fifteen or sixteen playing in rotation, a basketball, a couple of hockey nets, and, for each player, a cut-down worn-out straw curling broom with sweeping straws removed. For extra weight, the stub on the end of the broom was soaked in water for days on end. This gave the broom more "oomph" when striking the ball. And the rules of broomball were equally simple. All a player had to do was run the length of the surface of the arena, hitting the ball, hopefully into the other team's net, without falling prostrate and winded, gasping for air facedown on the concrete floor of the arena. Bodily contact, for obvious reasons, was not allowed unless one tripped accidentally over an exhausted participant lying on the playing surface.

My team was the high school team, made up of boys and girls. As we were younger, we certainly had more stamina, better legs, and cleaner lungs than the older cigarette-infused teams. On one occasion I shall never forget, we were playing our nemesis, the schoolteachers. Most of the older male teachers had smoked for years, and we students were undeniably in far better shape. However, the teachers' team also had a smattering of young female teachers who appeared quite athletic and were non-smokers. I had the feeling these girls were from farms, were healthy, and could easily beat us up.

During a game, I ran for a loose ball, attempting not to collide with an enthusiastic, athletic, very young, and very pretty farmer's daughter, perhaps only five years older than I. Her pace easily kept up with mine, and we both arrived at the ball at the same time. She took a swing at the ball, her straw less weighted broom performing a three-quarter semicircle. She missed the ball, but the broom continued its perfect arc. And she squarely hit mine. In plural. I collapsed in acute pain as she, red-faced, apologized profusely. My teammates were also doubled up with hoots of laughter, and I really, really hated them. I wildly wondered, in my panic, if my apparatus would ever work again. Of course, it did, as I later discovered to my delight. Again, all was well with the world.

And thinking of spring draws me to think of my old man, not that he was the kind of fellow one would look at and say, "Hey! My God! He looks like spring, don't you think?" No. Far from that! In many ways he looked like one of the most unspring-like fellows one could meet, especially as he, as we all inevitably must, grew older. Age plays cruel tricks on all of us—even on the most beautiful now, in the flower and vigour of youth.

My Dad could apparently see the future, like a druid wizard in ancient times or like the oracles of ancient Greece. And to prove it, not once but twice in a row, he accurately foretold the exact time of the official coming of spring in Churchill, virtually to the minute. How was this possible? Could he really see the future? Was he endowed with God-like supernatural powers? Much as I respected and sometimes feared the old man—almost as much as the Greeks feared the power of Zeus; the Romans, Jupiter; and the Vikings, Thor, with his angry hammer whacking away on his anvil—the long and the short of this is, of course, NO!

The old man loved challenges. He could use logic to escape a maze-like problem. And his memory was phenomenal. Let's get one thing straight. My old man was not well educated. Like most working-class boys, he and his contemporaries were ejected from school at fourteen to enter the working world. Child labour was then alive and well. He was placed in the trades, became a plumber, and, apart from the years of wartime service, remained a plumber. He was intelligent and scrupulous in his dealings. Oh, don't get me wrong; he liked a good deal as much as kids love birthdays and Christmas, but he always ended an agreement with a handshake, with both parties happy. He, almost with religious zeal, believed in honesty.

There was, in the mid-1960s in Churchill, a local service organization that raised money by selling tickets that allowed one to estimate the official time and date of the official breakup of the ice on the Churchill River. I was told that a barrel was placed on the ice of the river as a marker. The first continuous movement of the barrel marked the sign that the river ice was moving and sliding out toward the Bay and—Voila! —breakup and spring. The time was noted, the tickets perused, and the winning date and time won one hundred dollars; the second, fifty dollars; and the third, twenty-five dollars. Dad, who had paid his two dollars, wrote down the date and time—and won. He collected his cash winnings and promptly banked the money. He was always careful with cash that way. By the following year, I arrived home from university, and the contest to guess the time of breakup was once again in full swing. The old man bought a ticket, put down the date and the time, and told me to buy a time one minute after his, which I did. I was always an obedient child. I forked over my two dollars and wrote down the date and time suggested by Dad. And, sure enough, he won one hundred dollars for the second time in a row, and I won fifty dollars. I was delighted. Fifty dollars almost paid for one of my university courses. But then came the rumours and questions. How could George win twice? And in a row? And his kid won too? It was fixed—obviously. George had managed to accomplish the impossible. Or had he cheated? Yes. It was rigged. And that was that! Jealousy proved to be, once again, that green-eyed monster. Small towns can be mean like that.

The old man was incredulous. He was, as I said, a man of integrity. His handshake was his word. And he was so disgusted, he never bothered to buy a contest ticket estimating the time of the official ice breakup again.

Many years later, he and I were sitting on the deck of his cottage overlooking Georgian Bay. We each had a cold beer in hand, the sun was warm, life was pleasant, and he was contentedly enjoying retirement after over fifty years of work. The conversation somehow got around to Churchill and the great breakup controversy. "How did you do it?" I asked him. "Was it luck?" The old man chuckled and said he didn't believe in luck—not in the least. He believed in mathematics, playing the odds, and the probable. He was a statistician without training. Now here, I must say, that even playing cards with my dad was a nightmare. He knew which cards were to be played, who held what, and which cards had been played. His memory was phenomenal. He counted cards and, most certainly, would have been banned from Las Vegas casinos. He played the odds and won far more than he lost. Then he let me in on the truth regarding the movement of the ice on the Churchill River. He researched it. He hit the books and studied the tides. He knew exactly the date of the high tide and the time it would begin to ebb, causing the ice-laden tidal estuary to begin to move toward Hudson Bay. And from this, together with average-temperature charts and the past dates of breakup for support, he estimated the day, hour, and minute the marker barrel on the ice was likely to move. He estimated the probable. He used science, not guesswork nor the wife's birthday. And he happened to be correct. Twice. If he had tried a third attempt, he might have won again. If not, he would have been close. Somebody else might have won with sheer luck on his side, and the old man would have smiled and continued to play the odds, which were often in his favour, but he chose not to. And that, folks, is the story of how my dad foretold, accurately, the coming of spring in Churchill—twice—and how some said he had somehow cheated.

Summer in Churchill, in my memory, is a brief buzz of frantic activity. In a very short time, perhaps no more than ninety days, plants, animals, and birds must reproduce. Ships must arrive and depart. Belugas calve. Buildings come down and go up. Roads and roofs must be repaired. Long rows of rail cars must be marshalled and unloaded. All these activities must be accomplished in the warmth of the summer breezes and the twenty hours of daylight, activities that cannot be completed after the snow begins to fly, which I may add, I saw happen in every month except in July.

Thus it was in the summer, as I initially said, we kids ran free until our sixteenth birthdays when we were deemed old enough to drive and have a man's job in July and August, working for the Royal Canadian Engineers' Labour Shack, Pan American World Airlines—an airline that, for mysterious reasons known only to those with authority to know, operated the rocket launch facility for NASA, the US Air Force, and the Canadian Research Council—and finally, the National Harbours Board, where only dependents of employees seemed to get summer employment.

The Harbours Board did not directly hire the muscle to unload the ships' cargoes. These workers were hired by a company contracted by the Harbours Board to do the actual work, most of which was loading the ships' holds with wheat bound for Europe.

During the summer after finishing Grade 11, the government of Canada, as a way of saving money, decided to cut back on hiring part-time summer help, so there was little to be had in the way of summer employment. So, we tried our luck down at the docks.

A British freighter, we were told, was unloading cargo prior to loading up with wheat. As cargo rarely, if ever, came in through the port, extra hands would be temporarily needed to unload the vessel prior to loading. By six-thirty the next morning, there we were, standing, shivering in the biting chill coming off the water, huddled dockside, a small crowd of hopefuls grouped outside the hiring office. The cargo of the ship, rumour had it, was made up of Vauxhall cars, curling rocks, and Scotch whisky, and we were game to give it a good old-fashioned try. Eventually, two fellows emerged from the office and walked amongst us, eyeing us up and down. It was an unsettling experience, and I suspect I have a sense of how slaves in ancient Rome felt as they were to be put on the auction block and sold to the highest bidder, while the losers were sent to the Colosseum to be entertainment, eaten by hungry lions. These two fellows chose whom they wanted, wrote down the names of the chosen, and, if memory serves me as correct, gave each a numbered tag. Incredibly, despite being scrawny and weighing perhaps 125 pounds soaking wet, I was picked, along with Wayne. We attached the tags to our shirts, put on our leather work gloves, and were told we would be paid off in the evening—in cash. The work commenced immediately, and for those who had wintered without using the "work muscles" that had lain idle for ten months or so, it was hard—much harder than we imagined. The Vauxhall cars were packed in the cavernous hold of the ship and were lifted to dockside by crane to be put on flat cars and hauled south. This was, we were informed, the first and probably the only cargo of cars to be imported through the port, and they happened to be the easiest part of the day.

From the bowels of the ship next came granite stones—curling rocks, from Scotland with love—each rock weighing around forty pounds, three to a straw-filled wooden case that, itself, probably weighed ten pounds. So quick mental math said each case was at least 130 pounds, and there were dozens and dozens and dozens of cases, all destined to entertain winter work–adverse grain farmers in Saskatchewan, who would keep in winter shape by throwing or sweeping rocks down a long sheet of ice. Handling the first few boxes of rocks was okay, but at around the fortieth case, I could barely move. And it wasn't yet anywhere near noon, and we were expected to work until the cargo was emptied and the ship made ready to take on a load of wheat that evening and leave with the tide on the following day.

Along with the cargo of endless crates of rocks was whisky, a spirit often consumed on the rocks, but on that day, the wrong kind of rocks accompanied the whisky. The whisky was just more cargo to be removed. I had never, in my short life, seen so much alcohol in one place. There were boxes and boxes of it. At the time, being just sixteen, I was not such a Scotch drinker and, I may add, neither was my father. I was, consequently, schooled in the names of the products that left the ship, all heading to Saskatchewan, again to help winter work–averse grain farmers pass those long winter nights while casting those forty-pound chunks of granite down long sheets of ice. We, under the watchful eye of customs, loaded the boxes onto trolleys pulled by small gasoline-powered tractors. The Scotch was then taken directly to rail box cars, loaded, and counted. The car was then sealed, again by customs, ready to transport.

I do recall that, in the afternoon, one of the trains of trolleys, being pulled by an overly enthusiastic driver across the floor of the receiving hall where we were working, turned over as the driver attempted a turn at too high a speed. Boxes of Scotch fell from the trolleys, and pools of Scotch formed where bottles had broken. Immediately, the Revenue Men were there and sealed the area until all the broken and intact bottles were accounted for. Government bureaucracy had to be satisfied, even amid broken glass and swiftly evaporating pools of imported spirits. We were paid off in the early evening and told not to come back on the following morning. I was not too disappointed as I had never worked so hard for a bit of spending money. I found working for a private contractor to be much harder than working for the Canadian government or even Pan American. And shortly after, the government of Canada came to its senses, in Churchill at least, and decided that, after all, we summer-hire part-time hirelings were needed to shovel gravel and sand from one pile to another; otherwise, we would be one of the old man's "idle hands" prophesies and just get into trouble and possibly be a burden to government in other ways. It was cheaper to hire us than not.

Thus, from the time I was in Grade 10 until the very last summer job I really needed in order to pay for tuition, books, housing, and transportation at university, I worked. Summer was a time of labour, a time of learning and apprenticeship where life's lessons became reality. I learned how to dig graves; how to blow out asbestos-laden brake linings with an air hose; how to box and number items in a warehouse; how to drive a forklift and Ford Econoline vans; how to operate gas-powered compressors; how to purchase items from suppliers; how to calculate hours worked by a crew so they could be paid; how a Men's Mess fed 500 at a time; how to make coffee in huge urns for 500 coffee-deprived men at a time; how to sweep floors with endless bags of Endust; how to load a commercial movie projector at the local theatre; how to carry a clipboard, wander around, and look busy; how to peck at a typewriter; how to make forms for concrete, pour concrete, and remove forms from concrete; how to construct a simple building: how to shingle and hot tar a roof; and how to crawl in utilidors and service sump pumps. I learned how to use company time to get a haircut. After all, it grew on company time. I learned how to leave a jobsite at 4:30 p.m.so that I could get back, wash, and be in line to punch out at 5:00 p.m. And if I was early, I would go to Dad's shop and look busy, moving things around in one of the cupboards. I learned how to never admit to seeing something that you more than likely did see—should questions be asked. And I learned how to be "one of the guys," a man working with other men, even though I was just sixteen or seventeen. That was my Churchill summer. Perhaps the most wonderful and, insofar as seasons are concerned, the briefest season was summer. Summer represented freedom, the beginning of financial independence. Perhaps it was this that my dad wanted me to learn and, in turn, pass it on to my boys.

Of all the seasons then, I remember most the long days of summer, although I must confess that the girl-strewn autumn opening day of school in September, that wonderful Tuesday, the day after the Labour Day Monday, the first day of my new year, comes in as a very close second—especially with summer work cash deposited in the bank.

ANOTHER BRICK IN THE WALL

When the time arrived for me to attend high school in the late '50s, we "townies" had a problem. The Churchill townsite had no high school. Consequently, we who aspired to struggle around the academic racetrack and graduate from secondary school had two choices. Either we left town and travelled, on the parents' dime, 1,000 kilometres to a suitable school in the balmy south, or else, and I must assume some sort of financial agreement was struck permitting this, we registered with the school in Fort Churchill, an uncomfortable, bumpy bus ride down a pothole-riddled gravel road in a dilapidated, well-worn school bus, which on more than one occasion stalled and left us stranded with nothing to do than shiver and wait for the arrival of a replacement from town.

The Department of National Defence, as it did on most military bases, owned and operated the school in Fort Churchill for the education of military dependants living on the base. We townies felt we were permitted to attend as an afterthought. There was a sense that we were allowed to register simply because the administration had no choice in the matter—a sort of Hobson's choice—but they would have been far happier had we just stayed in town, where we belonged. We certainly lived on the wrong side of the tracks, down the highway where there was no running water, no sewers, nor paved streets. That was indeed how we felt, right or wrong.

This high school taught the basic curriculum designed for students who aspired to attend a post-secondary institution but provided no additional courses for those non-academics who looked for more than the basics. There was no art nor drama, no home economics nor industrial arts, no typing nor office skills, no biology, and certainly no guidance nor counselling. It offered just enough so that a graduate could apply to a university, a school of nursing, or a community college—all accomplished with little help from the school.

However, despite the lack of a comprehensive curriculum, this school bathed in the warmth of a name of not just ordinary repute. Experience tells me that many schools are named for a street on which they are located or in honour of a prominent citizen, war hero, educator, or even, and I find this hard to swallow, a politician. But my school, in that distant, faraway corner of subarctic Manitoba, basked in the golden glow of royalty, or as close to royalty as one could marry into. It was named in honour of the husband of the young sovereign, Queen Elizabeth, and carried the title "The Duke of Edinburgh School." Of this I am certain and have my doubts. I have my doubts that Prince Philip ever visited his namesake or was aware of its existence—or ours. If he was, he never said. And he never sent us a Christmas card.

Despite its royal connection, I must tell you that this school did no favours for my less scholastically inclined friends. It was a fact: few of the kids from town with whom I started high school, in Grade 10, graduated. The lack of interest in going to class and learning stuff that had no relevance to them, plus the siren call of easy money and low unemployment, had me see reasonably good kids, who could have attended a school that catered to their intellectual needs, come in and say, "Screw this . . . I'm off," then leave school and go to work. For them, going to school, at least that school, fitted them like a badly made suit. And there was, of course, no other local school within a sensible distance, and going off to another school, far from home, and boarding with a friend or relative, was next to impossible. They were between the proverbial academic rock and a hard place.

And while still on the topic of the guys who left school to work and earned enough money to buy that new car or truck that had perhaps twenty miles of unpaved, pothole-riddled road to drive on, well, those guys may have been flush with money, but we, still in school, had the pauper's advantage of actually being in close proximity to the girls that those working guys rarely saw when shovelling sand and gravel from one pile to another. We could perhaps be a row or two or, if lucky, one or two desks away from someone who happened to be our dream-girl crush for that hour, day, week, or month. A fifteen- or sixteen-year-old male is fickle indeed, and interests came and went so rapidly that today's creamy dessert quickly became yesterday's cold mashed potatoes. And who wants yesterday's cold mashed potatoes when a new dish of creamy dessert was put on the table? And, to add delicious frosting to the cake platter, there was always, annually, like Christmas but in September, when school reopened after the summer holidays on that wonderful Tuesday after Labour Day, a fresh crop of ponytailed, bobby-socked female arrivals who had descended upon Churchill in July and August, with the ebb and flow of the tide of military families moving predictably from one posting to the next.

My friends and I were, at that time in our lives, emerging as young men, all swimming in a sea of hormones, and we were, to say the least, interested in girls. But as we each had no car nor truck, and little money, all of which our non-academic friends who shovelled gravel and sand seemed to have, we aped Brando. We wore tight T-shirts, with the compulsory pack of twenty cigarettes in the left sleeve, and our equally tight blue jeans—at least as tight as our mothers would allow. We greased down our hair, until I got a brush cut on the stern suggestion of my dad. And, just to complete the masculine look, we wore black army surplus paratrooper boots, purchased by mail from the Army and Navy Surplus catalogue in Winnipeg. Unfortunately, these boots were promptly removed upon entering the school by order of the custodian, as the soles, he crustily claimed, left black skid marks on the floor. As for the cigarettes, this school, like most, had a sensible policy, frowning on students who flaunted cigarettes in the building. They would be immediately confiscated and, we were positive, later enjoyed by the teachers relaxing in the blue-tinged air of the staff room, a room permeated with cigarette smoke and the smell of coffee stewed in the pot for far too long. To prevent confiscation, the twenty-pack of cigarettes was slipped from the left sleeve of the T-shirt into the toe of the paratrooper boots we were told to remove, hidden from the prying eyes of the staff member in control of the 8:50 a.m. mayhem as we stormed the doors of the school. The boots and cigarettes were then safely stored in our lockers.

Every weekday, we waited for the bus in the town square at 8:15 a.m., hoping the bus was on time, which it frequently wasn't. Upon arrival, the bus rolled into the square, near the Hudson's Bay Company store, and parked near the flagpole. There were three things of note about the flagpole. First of all, atop the flagpole continually fluttered a tatty Red Ensign. Secondly, two ancient cannons that appeared to have no known owner, guarded the flagpole and the tatty Red Ensign. And thirdly, surrounding the flagpole was a circle of similarly sized rocks, all foolishly painted white by some enthusiast, a perfect trap for the unsuspecting after the first snowfall.

The bus service was such that one could reliably not set your watch by it. Frequently, the bus was late because it broke down or failed to start, especially in the deep chill of winter, and when this happened, we froze together in a pathetic, huddled group in the main entrance of the closed Hudson's Bay store. And although our parkas had perfectly functioning hoods, no man worth his salt would deem to pull it over his head and over his ears. Instead, we stood in the lee of the wind in the doorway of The Bay and held an occasional gloved hand to the part most likely to next turn white. To us boys, it was a pissing contest to see who would chicken out first and who, in the case of lasting the longest, somehow would prove his manhood.

There was a bakery and a coffee shop near the bowling alley and movie theatre, and the smell of fresh coffee and baking was irresistible. Some mornings would find us escaping the cold and crowding into the confined customer area to buy a fresh jam buster. And other times, we would "miss" the bus and, having an hour to kill, enjoy that jam buster with a coffee. The coffee, always served in sturdy, white china mugs, was adjusted to our immature tastes with at least two spoonfuls of sugar and a liberal pouring of evaporated milk We would then catch the 9:15 a.m. bus, pay two bits for the privilege, go to school, and report to the office late or better yet, no bother to go to school at all and wander over to Norm's for the day. There, we'd play cards, play the radio, play the record player, and play truant for the entire day in splendid manly companionship.

If on the following day a parental note was demanded by the teacher to explain our absence, we'd simply reply, "Forgot it, sir," or "Sorry, tomorrow, sir?" We found that eventually the teacher, who frequently had a rowdy class to work with, would give up. And that, as they say, was that! And on the day of our absence, there was no phone call from the school to my mother enquiring if little Johnny was not well and whether he perhaps would be well enough to attend school the following day. For all the school knew, I could have been in a ditch, half-consumed by a half-ton of giant white bear.

A fair question to ask at this time is, If I was ready to play hooky or "miss" the bus only to arrive at school late after a coffee and a doughnut, what was it that caused me to usually catch that bus, day after day?

First and foremost, there was my dad. Nothing on earth would shake him from making sure I got something he had no opportunity to receive—an education. I was allowed no debate in this issue. Period! Full stop! Second, I quite liked school most of the time. It was warm there, my day was organized, many of my friends were there, and I really hated manual labour. Summer work, toiling out of the aptly named "Labour Shack," had successfully convinced me there was no way I would spend my working life with a shovel or a pick or—God forbid—a jackhammer attached to an equally ear-splitting gasoline-powered compressor. Third, despite my struggles with mathematics and science, I gravitated like a fish to water toward English, history, and geography. And insofar as history was concerned, Churchill was the perfect home for me. There, I was surrounded by the vestiges of over 250 years of European colonial history in stone, bricks, and mortar, and the history of that financial colossus dominating the story of early Canadian history, the Hudson's Bay Company. And, thinking back sixty years, we had most of this to ourselves—tourists rarely ventured north.

For two years, my homeroom was the science lab. This room was supervised by an amicable fellow who failed, despite his best efforts, to pass on his obvious affection for either chemistry or physics. Our homeroom teacher was married to an elementary school teacher, who practised her skills in the elementary classrooms on the ground floor. Oh, how we envied him. She was a knockout. How, we wondered, did he manage to land such a beautiful, prize-winning trophy? It was love, I surmised.

And occasionally, to entertain us and teach us about physics, our teacher would haul out his banjo and play it for us. He was impressively good, plucking away at the strings. His performance, however, did not awaken any real interest in me regarding the physics of frequencies and the production of sound. His wife—and this is pure conjecture on my part—must have been impressed with his plucking ability. Why else, I ask myself, would such a delicious creature have agreed to marry him?

To entertain ourselves, when left alone in the classroom-cum-lab, we would catch flies batting themselves senseless against the windows, trying to escape to the outside world, and we would carefully drop them into the glass carboy of sulphuric acid on the lab's counter. We'd then make bets to see which fly lasted the longest as they darted between the acid and the hole we dropped them in. I'm not too sure which fate was worse for the fly: a shot of the old man's ample supply of US Army DDT or the carboy of sulphuric acid? Given a choice had I been a fly, my preference would have been the acid. It was instantaneous, unlike the lingering twitches brought on by DDT as the fly lay legs-up on the windowsill.

I recall that as a rare treat, our class was shown a NASA-produced movie, lauding the Americans' efforts to conquer space but conveniently omitting how all of those Nazi–war criminal scientists were forgiven as long as they worked toward Kennedy's promise to have a man on the moon before the end of the decade. The film showed enormous rockets rising, and many splendidly exploding in flames as they left the launch platform, but then it moved on to a successful launch where the rocket rose with a roar and with what appeared to be chunks of ice falling from it as it slowly lifted. The camera lens, in an obvious pulse of tribal pride, followed the letters *USA* as the rocket accelerated to a crescendo of patriotic music. Once the movie ended, our teacher, whom we boys would have probably followed to hell and back on the beaches of Normandy in 1944, spoke—probably without thinking—but spoke what many might have been thinking. He said he thought science was unfairly being used as propaganda, just as the Soviets used their achievements for propaganda. He referred to the letters *USA* so prominently featured on the screen. This, he hinted, was an abuse of science.

Suddenly, a girl in our class, an American girl with the soft drawl of a southern belle, burst into tears and fled the room, while we looked on in astonishment. We all assumed she had gone home as I don't recall seeing her for the rest of the day. How we would have loved to have been at that meeting that we all conjectured must have happened that day or evening between the principal, the parent, and the teacher over this issue. After all, we had long learned that Americans were understandably a wee bit touchy over any perceived insults, and our science teacher had apparently found and poked at one by what he had said.

I trudged on through Grade 11, thoroughly enjoying my history and English classes and slogging away at chemistry, physics, and mathematics. By

Grade 12, having passed some subjects by the skin of my teeth, I faced the torment of the same tortuous courses, especially math and physics. I had by then concluded that I would never be a Newton or an Einstein or a Faraday, but I could be a writer, a historian, or, at the very least, a teacher. Therefore, I dropped physics and persuaded the old man to part with the cash so that I could take "The History of Western Civilization," by myself, by correspondence. Despite his skepticism, he agreed. With that hurdle cleared, I could then concentrate on the horrors of mathematics, and I can honestly say that I gave it a good effort and that I had tried.

Our Grade 12 math teacher was also our principal, and he apparently enjoyed two things when teaching math. The first was to give a test, without fail, every Friday afternoon. The second was to return the tests on Monday, in my case, covered with so much red ink, the paper looked decidedly blood-stained. And believe me. If, like me, you were weak in math, Monday was not the day you would look forward to. Oh, Friday evenings were okay, three days to Monday. I tolerated Saturday, two days to Monday. When Sunday dawned, with one day to go to Monday, I honestly contemplated going with Mother to the evangelical church—for divine intervention, I suppose—but elected not to go and found myself on Monday wishing I had attended the service, as I needed all the intervention, divine or otherwise, I could get. But I will say this. Although I hated the whole process, the principal persevered and pushed enough mathematical mumbo jumbo into my head so that I scraped by my final math exam. Hallelujah! So, thank you! Without those well-marked tests, I probably would not have passed.

As my interest and skills in math were so awful, I elected to abandon physics in favour of a history course, which I did reluctantly because the new high school physics teacher was female, around twenty-two years old, single, and very attractive. I envied those guys who stuck with physics. Oh, how I envied them, but I knew that my chances of passing were remote and, with such a pretty teacher, nonexistent. The problem for me was that this history course was not taught at that school. As a result, Dad sent the correspondence branch a cheque, a sum I do not recall, enrolling me in the course with the caveat that if I passed the exam, the fees were refunded to the old man. If I failed, I was a dead man. In this way, the correspondence branch utilized my fear in combination with a carrot and a stick. Thereafter, whenever there was a physics class and my classmates trooped off to the wonderful world of Newton's apple and the pretty teacher, I was to use that time to independently study my history and write and send in my assignments and tests. I was left for the first time ever to study fully alone, free to work diligently and independently. Of course, tasting academic freedom for the very first time, I chose only the "freedom" part. I used the unsupervised periods to enjoy the fruits of youth. In the idle playground of my mind, I daydreamed, especially about girls, and more than especially about Linda in white short shorts. And as it does, time slipped by effortlessly, quickly. The end result? As an Easter present around March, the old man received a letter from the principal stating that he, in turn, had received word from the correspondence branch that I had, in turn, ignored warnings from the correspondence branch that I was behind in my history tests and assignments. And if I did not catch up soon, I was out of the course, and the old man would forfeit the cash that he in good faith had paid for me to take the course in the first place. And, if there was anything the old man hated even more than paying taxes, it was the complete waste of hard-earned cash.

He called me "boy" in his initial remarks about my study habits. He called me "boy" only when he was angry with me. He made it clear that either I got off my behind and got to work on my history course, or I would get off my behind, get a job, and go to work. Period! Facing reality, I got to work on my studies. I laboured not only during school hours when all my other classmates merrily romped off to physics class, and the pretty physics teacher, but I laboured after school and at home, catching up on work previously ignored. And in three months, I managed to finish all tests, all assignments, and not only pass the examination but also earn the highest mark of all the exams I wrote that June.

And as for my old man . . . he was still mad at me but was happy because he got his money back, money a short time prior he had seen evaporating because of my laissez-faire attitude. And he kept the refund. There was no, "Here, boy. Here's ten bucks for your efforts." That simply did not happen. And to be truthful, after all the crap I had put him through, I did not deserve it.

The best part of my school day—as well, probably, for the frazzled teachers who had to put up with us—was the lunch hour. Come the noon-hour siren, which radiated out around Fort Churchill like a call to freedom, we were ushered out onto the streets by the staff and left to our own devices as to where our lunches were to be consumed. On those warm early September days, we may have moved down to the rocks and eaten while watching the grain ships riding at anchor as we debated the nationality. British? Norwegian? Russian? You could always tell the Russians. Their ships looked different—like floating radar stations. There was always a United Nations of vessels out there, arriving and then departing port. Or we followed them, with fingers pointed at the pilot in his tiny boat as it scudded around the river estuary, like a collie herding sheep, leading the freighters to dockside. But most of the time, especially as the weather closed in and the days swiftly cooled, we would run to the warmth of the engineers' canteen. It was there our dads, off work for an hour, would have their noon-hour lunch break, and we joined them. Out from the doors of the school we'd run, largely ignoring the pleas of the supervising teacher to "slow down, boys." We'd run across the street, past the Sergeants' Mess to G Area, a long string of Permanent Married Quarters (PMQs) with each block of PMQs connected by a heated corridor. Down the corridor we'd go, carelessly banging open the steel fire doors that separated each block of housing, lucky that no one was behind one of those doors as each slammed open, while we acted, as boys do, like horses' patoots. Within ten minutes, we navigated the maze from the school down the hallway, cutting through the G Area PMQs. Then we continued outside past the petrol point and the motor pool, past the enormous heavy equipment garage, and then to the Royal Canadian Engineers' stores where the old man stashed his plumbing supplies, along with the bric-a-brac of all the trades. And then, it was a sharp left toward the engineers' shops and the Works Canteen. There, in the company of painters, plumbers, electricians, and carpenters, we settled behind the long bench tables. We ordered a can of soup from Mrs. Taylor, who always stood smiling from behind the counter. She was a very jovial lady. "A cream of mushroom soup, please, Mrs. Taylor." When it was heated, we took the soup can to the table and then added a splash of evaporated milk, always in plentiful supply in cans on the table. Then along with the soup and sandwiches came the real education of the day. These tradesmen, many of whom were World War II or Korean War veterans, ate and played cards. And, like any good soldiers, they taught us and sometimes took us at cards. We learned the finer points of poker: to count cards; to work the odds; to know when to say, "I'll see you," "Raise you a nickel," or "I'm out"; or, most importantly, how to put on a blank stare and bluff. We played mostly for pennies or, in my dad's case, with matchsticks because his favourite game was racing them around a cribbage board, a board that, I must tell you, I still have at home.

Time has passed like a breeze, invisible but tangible—especially evidenced when I look at the bathroom mirror at my reflection each morning. Yet despite that aging face and creaky limbs challenged by a flight of stairs, I find my mind back in that bygone, youthful world, when nimble feet took me, chasing from the school, down corridors, slamming open fire doors without a pause, never thinking that a child might be playing there on the other side. Luckily, there never was. Those years were the years that the foundation upon which lives—my life and the lives of my friends—were built. And the architects? Our parents, who loved us unconditionally. The teachers at that school I attended most of the time, who did try to push some of the residue of Western civilization into our heads. The girls, who demonstrated to us boys that there was an alternative feminine point of view we should consider. Our summer employers in those summer months of employment, who proved to us that money did not simply grow on trees; it had to be earned. And most of all, my dad. A man of quiet wisdom who would tell me, "Son, you can work with these," as he held up his work-worn hands, "or this," and he pointed to his head. "Your choice, boy." Words of wisdom any son in any family could live by.

And there it is. By the mid-'60s, I had two degrees and followed the natural progression of work, play, marital bliss, and debt. And to think, it all began in that small high school, miles from any other high school, the school with that pompous name that, like everything else I grew up with, was destined to meet the blade of the bulldozer. Now all that remains are the memories. And for that I am hugely grateful.

SUMMER VACATION—THE HIGH
SCHOOL YEARS, 1959-1962

The summers that marked the years after my sixteenth birthday were not exactly those lazy days of summer we conjure in our minds, spent sleeping, relaxing, or lazing on recliners working on the perfect tan. The fact was, with my sixteenth birthday in late May, I was considered old enough at sixteen to go to work every July and August. After writing my last exam in June, there I was, together with several of my similarly blessed contemporaries, my classmates, in line, in the employ of the Royal Canadian Engineers—in line with my timecard to punch in on the time clock and in line with the tradesmen who worked out of the trades' shops. These were the guys who kept the base going: the electricians, the plumbers, the carpenters, and the painters. They kept the lights on, kept the toilets and taps running, patched and painted the walls, and were the elite of the workforce. I, however, did not work out of those trades' shops. No. The tribe I joined for eight or nine weeks were the labourers, a singularly unskilled group who manned the shovels, picks, and spades, who dug holes and then filled them in again, or were called upon because of their young bodies or strong backs to pile, move, and then pile once again countless bags of cement powder. Once I punched in, I wandered to the Labour Shack, a nondescript annex, separate from the trades' shops and attached, as in afterthought, to the rear of the Works Canteen. The Labour Shack had a very small office where the foreman, known by all as Scotty—presided over the fiefdom. It was there that the labour crew ignored the "NO SMOKING, DÉFENSE DE FUMER" sign attached to the wall, claimed spots, and sat on benches around the perimeter. Those who did not claim a spot on one of the benches either sat on the floor or leaned indolently against the wall, all awaiting the daily work orders. Often, two or three large army lorries idled and rumbled near the door of the Labour Shack, waiting to transport crews and their tools to various work sites.

The daily work orders for some were easy and coveted, say sweeping the floors of the huge, corrugated steel quonset huts (which were used to house lumber or trades' supplies) or, better yet, assigned as a temporary helper to a trades' shop to assist the plumbers, carpenters, or electricians. By definition, a helper was little more than a tool caddy for the tradesman, carrying and handing him the right tool for the occasion. Innocent sixteen-year-olds, like me, were sent to the stores, which warehoused a huge variety of specialized tools, to requisition a "left-handed monkey wrench, please," only to be told by a clerk there to "buzz off and stop wasting my time." Yes, indeed, we were truly innocent and eager. My very first responsibility was being sent for a week to the motor pool. There, as if desperate to find anything for me to do, I was handed a high-pressure hose with a trigger attached to squirt a danger-ous, high-pressure, skin-removing stream of compressed air, supposedly at the brake drums of vehicles. But as these were often in short supply, and I endured moments of infinite boredom, I created targets. I blew stray pebbles across the concrete floors to see how far they would go. I blew air at assorted bits and bobs, especially pieces of paper that, I learned, float in the air for prolonged periods of time. Or, if one came into view, I blew air at a housefly that might have landed on a truck's bumper or on the concrete floor. And, if you were wondering, or perhaps not, those occasional brake drums I blew out were loaded with asbestos fibres. We, at the time, knew nothing about the dangers associated with inhaling asbestos—or were simply not told by those who did know but chose not to say. Fortunately, I seem to have escaped the consequences of floating airborne asbestos particles. I am lucky, unlike so many others.

Following the week of boredom at the motor pool, I was told to board a truck, together with half a dozen others, and spent a week shovelling gravel and sand and lifting and piling bags of cement, with every muscle in my then skinny body crying with pain with every movement. Even lying in bed after a date with a shovel was a painful experience. Then on Friday afternoon, as the week concluded, Scotty appeared at the site in his ancient army panel van.

He cornered me and, in his thick, almost impossible to understand Scottish brogue, informed me he had a special job for me on Monday that would probably last all week—longer if it rained.

"Aye laddie," he said, "make sure ye pack a lunch and thermos, aye, there's somethin' special for ye."

I should have realized that when he said "special," it was indeed "special," especially when he ended with a smile.

That weekend, my old man, who rarely—no, I must correct that—who never took much of an interest in my day-to-day routine, asked me how work was going. I replied that Scotty had made a somewhat cryptic remark about a "special wee job" and to bring my lunch and thermos on Monday to the Labour Shack. My old man said nothing, but I did notice that his face lit up. He then left the kitchen by the side door, and I swear I heard him outside suppressing snorts of laughter.

On the Monday morning, after the Labour Shack emptied and I was the only one still there, Scotty called to me.

"Come here, laddie, aye."

He then put a reassuring arm around my shoulders and led me to the door. "Aye, we've got a wee job for ye, aye, we have. Come wi' me, laddie."

To be honest, whenever he spoke, I could hear the swirl of the pipes over the heather. I followed him out to the rear of the Labour Shack where his ancient Canadian Army panel van was parked, a vehicle held together by the rust that ran riot on its surface. Attached to the van was a gasoline-powered compressor, and in the back of the van sat two Inuit gentlemen who, I quickly discovered, spoke as much English as I did Inuktitut. Scattered between these two fellows was an assortment of well-worn tools, a jackhammer, and hoses. Both Inuit fellows, it became apparent, smiled no matter what, no matter the situation. And, at that moment, they both grinned and seemed to know something I did not.

Pulling on the once-chromed handle of the van's passenger side door, it reluctantly groaned open for me on well-worn hinges. I then settled my backside into a non-cushioned pit that once had been a seat where, over the years, numerous backsides had deposited themselves. Hauling his door to a reluctant, noisy close, Scotty looked at me and turned the key. The engine sputtered and, with a determined push on the clutch pedal, followed by the grinding of gears trying to desperately mesh, the van, passengers, tools, and compressor were off down the rough gravel road that connected Fort Churchill to the townsite. But to where exactly? He had not said, and he wore the mask of a secret smile that, frankly, appeared to grow with each passing bumpy mile.

As the van, like a great carnival ride concocted by a sadist, banged and jolted its way down the road, I began to smell in the air and in the smile on Scotty's face the growing presence of my old man. He and Scotty were friends, at least as close to being friends that a canny Scot and an Englishman could be. I began to hear voices, strong English, and Scottish voices, hear the plot in my mind that my old man cooked up with him.

"Scotty," I imagined him saying, "teach young Johnny the value of going to school."

My old man, like most immigrants, valued education as the way up the social ladder and worried about his children's educational aspirations.

"Give him one of the . . ." and here, in my mind, he searched for appropriate words. He then found them, ". . . most unpleasant jobs you can find. Make his life . . ." and here in my mind's ability to guess what was actually said, he again grasped for the appropriate words. He found them. "Make his life working a pick and shovel bloody miserable."

And then I could hear laughter and Scotty sputtering, "Aye, Georgie. I'll gi' the wee laddie the best I can find for ye," followed by yet more gales of laughter. Well, that was the way I imagined it, and to be honest, I wasn't wrong!

Upon reaching the outskirts of town, the van veered to the right off the highway and rolled onward and upward toward the rocks, the Bay, and what we in town for no apparent sensible reason called Camp 10, where the local Indigenous wards of the federal government were forced to live. This was an awful, windblown scattering of Indian Affairs housing that really belonged in the third world, not in Canada in the mid-twentieth century.

At the time, I had little contact with the folks who lived in Camp 10. They were different, and I truly believed they chose to live up there, on the wind-swept rocks overlooking the bay and the graveyard, and we, of course, didn't. And that, in my mind at the time, was that! That was the way, back then, things were. Cultural and racial lines were drawn, lives were separate, lines rarely crossed. They were them and we were us. Few questions were asked.

The van rolled on past Camp 10 and stopped with a squeal of brakes on the windswept gravel ridge that only a madman could conceive was a perfect place to locate either a cemetery for the dead or a settlement for the living.

And, not to put too fine a point on it, we were there that morning to work for the dead at the cemetery, and the living were once again abandoned to desperately exist in their shanties that faced the graveyard.

There was little to indicate this was a cemetery, the final resting place for many of the citizens of Churchill who (a) made the mistake of living and then dying in Churchill and (b) probably had no intention of spending eternity there, but there they were. Forever! Scotty told us that we were to prepare half a dozen new graves, graves to give those already in repose their new company. Yes, we were to dig new holes in the ground, holes made ready for new occupants who were going to die but apparently didn't know it yet.

The coffins I had, by chance, already seen were lovingly constructed from the very finest grade of plywood in the carpenter's shop by Fred, who informed me that people were just dying to get into them. He laughed heartily at this joke. He quite honestly took great pride in making those plywood boxes look as presentable as possible, using the very best brass handles, stains, and lacquers. He was a craftsman indeed.

The spot Scotty had parked on was within the cemetery boundaries. He coaxed open his door, got out, and surveyed the premises. An amateur surveyor had already marked outlines for the new graves, and our task was simple: excavate the stuff within the lines that marked the new gravesites. To make that task easier, the two Inuit workers had industriously removed the assorted tools from the panel van and unhooked the compressor. Shovels, picks, and spades lay on the ground, followed by—the most formidable tool I had seen—the jackhammer and its hoses, which were attached to the compressor by the two Inuit gentlemen. They obviously knew what they were doing. All the while, they smiled and occasionally gave me a knowing wink. If it had been left to me, I would have had no clue what to do.

Scotty pointed out to us what had to be done. This was accompanied by nods and more smiles from the Inuit fellows and a hopeless shrug from me. I had absolutely no idea whatsoever how to dig a grave. Then he rumbled off in his van, telling me he'd be back and leaving me on that windswept, rock-strewn rise with a compressor, jackhammer, and my new colleagues, neither of which I understood.

At first it was easy. We worked together, loosening the surface with a pick and spades, and piling the spoil on one side. Slowly, the hole grew deeper; the pile, higher; and the loose rocks and stones, less loose as we reached the level of permafrost, about a foot or so below the surface. Here, the pick was swung by one as the stones flew, and after a few minutes, the two with spades attacked the loosened material. But progress was slow. Around ten o'clock, we took our morning coffee break, without coffee, just sitting on a small pile of newly uncovered stones that literally froze the bum if you sat for too long. I took advantage of the time to explore this area, a place I had never ventured to before, and wandered close to the houses of Camp 10 but was scared off by a husky baring his teeth at me. Luckily, the dog was attached to a stake by a rope. I determined that I would not want to wander around there at night, as I discovered that the locals habitually parked their dogs there, all attached to stakes by a rope, when the dogs were not in use. It was a sort of husky parking lot, and a lethal trap for unwitting hikers.

And these were the same dogs, I determined, we could hear howling a Hell's chorus at the new moon. Scotty reappeared, as promised, at noon to inspect the progress. It was slow, but being a civil servant in government employ, he appeared satisfied. Then, once again, he and his van sputtered off, with the promise he would return around four.

The afternoon was a repeat of the morning, and I even got a brief lesson, by sign language, on jackhammer operation. The noise was deafening but beginning to master a tool like a jackhammer gave me a sense of satisfaction. It was a milestone in the things a boy tends to do to prove his manhood— what a young man is driven to do to prove himself to himself. My personal list includes driving a friend's father's tractor, a John Deere, for the first time, right through a wire fence; tasting Scotch for the first time and wondering how anybody in the world could actually like that stuff; driving a car for the first time and being in awe of the power beneath the right foot; and most important of all, for a teenaged boy, kissing a girl for the first time and feeling like the conqueror Caesar crossing the Rubicon, knowing in both cases a real line had been crossed, an action that was impossible to take back. And although the brute force of a pneumatic jackhammer as it powered into permafrost, frozen stone, and gravel was impressive, that did not come even close to the soft, curvy playground of a girl. But it was still a momentary, seminal event in my young life that will always be with me—at least until my mind gives up or forgets, whichever comes first.

Sure enough, around four o'clock, Scotty reappeared in his panel van. We had an hour to collect our gear and pile it in the back of the van, disconnect the compressor from the hoses of the jackhammer, attach the compressor to the ball on the bumper of the ancient van, and then get back to the Labour Shack by 5:00 p.m. to punch out. All travel, even for the twice-daily twenty-minute coffee breaks, was on company time. This meant that an eight-hour day could easily be reduced to six hours.

Driving back that evening in the ancient '40s-era van, I barely heard the banging as the wheels hit potholes. The noisy jackhammer had been replaced by an annoying ringing sound. Even today, in my approaching dotage, I still hear a continual ringing, in stereo, in my head. I cannot ignore nor escape it, and my exasperated missus claims I am deaf, a claim I find hard to dispute, although she does speak, as I have often complained, far too softly.

Perhaps the noise of the jackhammer I experienced far too many years ago was partially responsible. All that I hope is that, in return for my ringing sound in stereo, the residents now relaxing in the solid comfort of one of Fred's handcrafted boxes are grateful for the efforts of two smiling, cheerful Inuit gentlemen and one now partially deaf Englishman.

Thankfully, after a couple of days of apprenticeship in the funeral business, I was pulled from grave production to the blissful silence of floor sweeping, on my own, with my brooms, in a series of quonset huts where assorted supplies were delivered, stored, picked up, and removed. Life was perfect until, within a week, my stint in the quonset huts all alone, in the blissful silence, ended as it had begun, and I was assigned a new role, a role I was to dislike for several reasons.

I was assigned to assist Mr. Coltrain, although after a short time, for the life of me, I seriously questioned why Mr. Coltrain required an assistant, as he was probably one of the slowest-working men I knew.

Mr. Coltrain was a lovely gentleman who, I believe, lived in a house on the Churchill River flats, on the other side of the CN yard, a place I rarely visited, as it was a part of town that scared me. He worked through my old man's shop, the plumber's shop, and spent his day, every day, for eight hours a day, for every week of his working life, crawling around the subsurface service world of shit, sewers, and pumps. His role was to ensure all the pumps were in working order and replace, repair, or service those that needed replacing or an overhaul.

But, lovely as Mr. Coltrain was, and he really was a true gentleman, he had a near-fatal flaw that drove people crazy. The flaw was, I believe, a product of years of solitary work, just him and his humming pumps for company. The flaw was, he whistled. He whistled tunelessly. He whistled constantly. He whistled all the time. And to think, I was to be trapped with this man's tuneless, musical solitary adventures for eight hours a day, for the rest of the summer, until September, trapped in tunnels and tiny low-ceilinged service utilidors.

His role was to ensure that all the sewer lines were working efficiently, taking the kitchen grey water, and mixing it with bathroom poop, paper, pee, condoms, and whatever else that could be flushed down a toilet and was then efficiently pumped to a sewer outlet that discharged untreated raw sewage into the tidal waters of the bay, and was hopefully never seen again. Mr. Coltrain apparently liked the leisurely subsurface pace of life as he slowly whistled his way around the hidden subterranean, underfloor maze of tunnels, pumps, and utilidors. He had, at strategic locations, created built-in leisure centres equipped with reading lights, a pile of magazines, and soft layers of cushions to recline upon as he contemplated life over his thermos of coffee and bag of cookies. Here he read, whistled, and, in between, sipped his beverage. And then, with a glance at his watch, he turned out the light and moved on to tackle the next pump. This job was, for me, mind-numbing, and I hated it. I am a gregarious person. I like to talk to people. I like their company. I love fresh air and crave open spaces. This job offered none of these. This job drove me crazy, along with the constant, tuneless whistling.

To add to my consternation about working there was the fact that the utilidors could be oppressively hot and were always narrow. Utilidors are concrete tunnels, no more than a claustrophobic three to four feet high and perhaps six feet wide, that we crawled through on our hands and knees. I began to appreciate how the new occupants of one of Fred's boxes would feel, except they would lie in a permanent natural cooler of permafrost, while I suffered from the heat of the utilidors. These structures carried the electrical cables, phone lines, water pipes, and sewer lines, and insulated hot pipes carrying calorie-laden heat in the form of steam from the steam plant to PMQs and other buildings. I sweated profusely and thirstily drank water whenever I found a tap. I lost weight. I sweated so that my T-shirts were soaked in perspiration, as was my underwear that I wore beneath those tight blue jeans that I considered to be sexy and Marlon Brando–like. But unlike Mr. Coltrain's baggy, sensible workpants, my jeans were totally unsuitable. After a few days, due, I suspect, to a lack of air circulation beneath my jockey shorts, my nether region became sore and inflamed. It was torment, and I was worried as I began to walk bowlegged, somewhat like John Wayne carrying a pair of six-shooters on his hips in some long forgotten western. Was it curable? How long would it last? Boys do tend to be sensitive about such sensitive problems in such sensitive areas. I was worried, so much so that I finally, in surrender, put my hands up and set off for the hospital to see a sympathetic army doctor who, after inspection, gave me some ointment and some sage advice.

"Wear boxers, boy" he said. "Let 'em swing free."

"And" he smiled, "for Christ's sake, wear looser jeans. Those'll just cook your balls!"

And since then, I have.

After a week following Mr. Coltrain, my only way out of the utilidors and pumps and sore, inflamed ball sac and the chronic whistling was to personally appeal to Scotty for an early release, to appeal to his better angels and plead with him to assign me elsewhere please, please. Anywhere. I'd do anything else, even graveyard work. I could've told him about my balls but, for reasons known only to me, I didn't. And in a moment of humanitarian weakness, Scotty relented and put me to work with my friend Wayne, on top of a huge pile of gravel at the Sergeant's Mess. Some of the guys thought I was crazy, and I never told them of the ointment and the boxer shorts. To be truthful, I was on top of a pile of gravel feeding a concrete mixer, doing a job I liked, with guys I quite liked, earning a paycheque I really liked. This job took me all the way to September and school, which, I must admit, I then tolerated and did not like. But I had money in the bank for the very first time, balls that felt normal, and new girls at school to charm. Life was indeed wonderful.

THE CORNERS OF MY MIND

Like most of us, I find myself ruminating at times on the morsels of memory that lie hidden in those infrequently visited, dimly lit corners and corridors of the mind. It was while idly wandering one of those corridors that I happened upon a door to a room, a door obviously long closed, bearing just the hint of a sign that read "School Days." I stopped, intrigued. I pushed at the door. Then slowly creaking on ill-oiled, long-neglected hinges, it opened upon a room, dusty from years of neglect. As my eyes adjusted to the light, I saw memories, like faded, flickering pictures, hanging from the walls. I was instantly reminded that I was not a particularly energetic student. I saw in those memories a youngster who knew how to work the system, do just enough to pass tests and exams, most of the time, but certainly never earned the teacher's gold star. I was, to be truthful, the kind of kid who sat on the proverbial gold mine but never bothered to find the effort to vigorously dig and become rich.

My parents, on the other hand, valued education. They had both been born English working-class, born near the bottom rung of the English social ladder, and saw education as a way for their children to climb that ladder. Their education had been basic and brief, and at age fourteen, they had been thoughtlessly tossed into the working world, a common practice for working-class children in the first half of the twentieth century. Thus, on her fourteenth birthday, my mother was sent from her rural home, a home packed with a tribe of brothers and sisters. She was ushered out to live in a rich Englishman's large country home, there to work as a scullery maid largely in exchange for room and board, as a servant who was, in the weird, class-ridden order of things then practised by the English downstairs-servant class, at the very bottom of the servant pecking order. It was there, in that house, she chanced upon a boy from the city, an apprentice plumber, and at the age of seventeen, happily escaped the drudgery of being a scullery maid by marrying that boy and producing my older brother in 1938.

As for that boy, my Father, he entered a trade he was to employ for the whole of his working life, less the seven years he was to spend in the army during the Second World War. Had he been given the chance to continue with his education, which he wasn't, he might have made a fine engineer or architect, or even a poet. He certainly had the mindset of an engineer and, unlike me, was a whiz at mathematics. But in his heart, he was a poet. As a youngster, I recall he listened, much to my dismay, to opera on his "radiogram"—a machine I was justifiably forbidden to touch—putting on one of his favourite Classic 33⅓ rpm vinyl records ordered through a mail in record company, sitting back, and closing his eyes as the sounds of Puccini or "Sunrise" from the *Grand Canyon Suite* filled the room. The closest that machine got to playing popular music was when Mother played one of her Johnny Mathis or Nat King Cole recordings and danced wistfully by herself on a quiet weekday afternoon, when she had the ballroom to herself.

So, as you can see, my parents were people who truly valued education, something denied to them. And to top it off, they landed with a lazy lunk like me. They urged me to complete high school and then hopefully go on to college or, even better, university. As the old man never tired of repeating, time and again, "You can work with these," and here he'd show his work-hardened hands, "or with this," and he'd point to his head. "Your choice, boy." I really believe that he believed people who used brains instead of brawn really didn't work. After all, they wore white shirts and had clean, uncalloused hands. And he was determined his sons would wear white shirts and enjoy the dignity of very clean hands. No excuses permitted!

Those character-forming teenage years saw me living in a community that lay literally at the far end of the Hudson Bay Railway line. My communication with the world at the other end, not to put too fine a point on it, was virtually nonexistent. I felt as though I were a resident of distant Pluto, looking toward a dim, faraway star—our sun. Meanwhile, the kid residing at the other end of the rail line in Winnipeg, on the planet earth, 1,000 kilometres to the south, had it all. There, the sun shone brilliantly. There, he had opportunities we Plutonians could only dream of. On earth, there were high schools that offered courses that were relevant to the needs of the students and, after high school, a university, and colleges of repute, made up of faculties I was vaguely aware existed. Yes, it was all there!

In contrast, at our end, the far end of the line, there was us, a relatively small band, residents of Pluto, about to write our final exams, being examined in subjects that, for many of us, were of virtually no interest nor educational relevance. We had an educational "Hobson's choice," a take-it-or-leave-it proposition put on the educational platter. And, living in a northern community where the take-it-or-leave-it philosophy was alive and well, where choices in almost anything were almost nonexistent, we took what was offered—or quit.

Furthermore—and I may be corrected here, but I believe my stop in the "School Days" room tells me this is true—no teacher, in fact, nobody at all, told us of the wonderful world of choices that lay waiting in the outside world. There was no visit by representatives of any institution of higher learning nor greetings from any professional organizations. No, nothing except, and this is indeed strange, a one-period sermon from the military Roman Catholic priest, who apparently did represent all three of the following: the Department of National Defence, the Pope, and God. He talked to the boys and girls separately, but the reason for his visit is long forgotten. Perhaps he was trying to reap a rich harvest of potential priests or nuns. But if so, he was wasting his time because, first, many of us were protestants, and second, we were all swimming in a sea of hormones. Consequently, the idea of celibacy was quite simply unthinkable.

The point I am trying to make is that nobody—absolutely nobody—posed the question, "Well now, boys and girls, what are you going to do with the rest of your lives now that we have finished filling your heads with pointless stuff, most of which you were probably never interested in and will certainly forget anyway shortly after you write your final exams?" Apparently, it seemed that once the school doors hit our backsides for the last time on the way out, we were to be set loose to fend for ourselves.

So what did happen to us "townies," residents of the townsite who, in the bitter cold of winter, rode the bus daily to and from the town square—with its flagpole flying the tattered Canadian Red Ensign, two ancient cannons guarding it, and the circle of craftily painted white rocks—to the two-sto-reyed vice regally named school inside of which an education was pushed into the vacant spaces between our ears?

Well, for one thing, many of the girls who rode with us and were our classmates in Grade 10 did not complete Grade 12 and left school. Where the girls disappeared to, I cannot say for sure, but I am confident that boys were a part of the equation.

And for another, many of the guys we chummed with had become bored with the school's academic offerings and had succumbed to the siren call of employers looking for young men with young bodies and strong backs to shovel gravel, wield heavy tools, or, if fortunate, drive a truck, front-end loader, or forklift. These were not skilled jobs but were well paid and immediate. What happened to these young men as these jobs evaporated and the young men aged, many with no real skills, I'll never know. But I was certainly envious of their ability to purchase new cars and trucks, their wallets stuffed with spend-ing money. And I was envious watching as the smiling girls who sat next to them in their new cars and trucks helped to separate these boys from the cash stuffed in their wallets.

There is another memory lingering in that room, flickering like a silent picture movie. There you see three sixteen-year-olds who lived for the moment, only vaguely aware of the fact that there was a life ahead to live. Three teenagers who had just been foolishly granted, by the powers that be in the province, the right to drive. Three teenagers who lusted after but did not have the financial resources to purchase a car, which they were certain would yield to them all the female company they desired. Three teenagers with fathers who owned cars but were wisely reluctant to allow them to cruise the town in the family car on a Friday evening, looking for available female companionship to impress with the borrowed family wheels.

Those three were close friends, but different in interest. Norm was the first to leave school in Grade 11. He was the most practical and became a stationary engineer at the steam plant and, of the three of us, was financially the most astute. I understand he did very well in investments later in life.

The second, Wayne, was the most scientifically minded of the three of us. It was with him that I made hesitant steps to attend university on the "outside," and once there, we roomed together until he met a girl and married her before graduation. As a youth, he subscribed to *Scientific American* and lent the copies to me, although I will readily admit most of the articles were beyond me and, I suspect, him too! He spent endless hours trying to figure out how to power rockets, and we liberated chemicals and equipment, in the ample folds and pockets of our parkas, from a school with very lax regulations on the availability of chemicals for just that purpose. Most of our attempts in rocket propulsion ended in a blaze of fire, a wonder to see but wholly unsuccessful. NASA would never call.

And then there was me. There, you see a young man who loved history, read biographies of the famous and infamous, who leafed through history books, regarding the content as a pleasure, not a toil, who explored the local presence of the Hudson's Bay Company in the neglected and crumbling ruins of eighteenth-century bric-a-brac, imperial ruins that predated the American Revolution, hand-hewn granite time machines that lay scattered near the community like the seeds of history waiting for somebody to take a scholastic interest in them, before nature and negligence took their toll.

Moving around the room there is yet another flickering memory where you can see two boys with fishing rods, wandering the rocky shore of the Bay. It is a fine June evening, far too pleasant to be indoors studying mathematics like most responsible students in the province. We had told our parents we were off to the other's house to study. Lies dripped from our lips like honey, a skill we attempted to perfect in our efforts to charm girls in the not-too-distant future. We would, we breezily told our parents, be home around ten. The parents apparently believed us. Most girls, sensibly, did not.

We had, until a few weeks prior, been stuck on the inside looking out at the snow swirl and whirl in unpredictable circles. Now, the evening beckoned. We fished off the docks and the beach, watching the ice that floated and broke apart and moved with the tides and the wind. And on the beach, abandoned by the tide, lay great chunks that yielded to the warmth of the sun and air, and shrunk by the hour as solid became liquid. In the open water, seals were out, chasing and feasting on fish that ran close to shore. And occasionally, one would pop to the surface, regarding us with curiosity until, with a great gulp of air, he disappeared. It was the most perfect of evenings, but not for math. As it was mid-June, the sun barely set. By ten, we both finally hurried home, in broad daylight, to parents oblivious of how we spent the evening.

But that night, I was strangely content and calm and slept well in my bed. Perhaps I was inhabiting a fool's paradise, but I felt the world was unfolding as it should. And the following day, I took the morning bus to school and wrote that exam. And despite the dour predictions of my teacher, or my wandering the shore that previous, perfect, profoundly beautiful evening, I passed. I passed not spectacularly but, in fact, by the skin of my teeth! How? Perhaps, by chance, there were problems and questions that I could take at least a half-hearted stab at solving. Or perhaps, and this is doubtful, I knew a wee bit more than either I or my teachers realized. Or, and this is what I really believe to be true, the exam consisted of the same problems I had understood, at least in part, and I was just plain lucky because my paper was given to a sympathetic marker who saw me as someone who, in the future, would only use math to read a tape measure or to compute change from a dollar. He saw me as someone who would never again use Grade 12 math or a slide rule because they would be totally irrelevant in my life. He saw me as someone who needed a seat in the lifeboat, and he took pity, knowing full well that engineering would never be my faculty of choice.

With the delivery of our final results in July, my high school years coasted to an end. There was no applause from proud parents or faculty, no "Land of Hope and Glory" banged out on an ancient upright piano as the graduates filed in. As a matter of fact, there was no graduation ceremony at all—no high school diploma; no graduation prom; no shy, corsaged girl wearing a formal dress; and no awkward boy in a tuxedo, both posing stiffly for pictures. All we possessed to prove this educational milestone were our marks, printed in triplicate, mailed in July. School concluded, not with a bang but with a soft, whispered sigh of relief. School, as the results showed, was out forever. By reason of laziness, lack of ambition, or anything better to do, university beckoned. And those years are to be found in memories hanging like pictures in dusty rooms located along dark cranial corridors elsewhere, waiting for the right moment to open the creaky doors and look inside.

TICKET TO RIDE, 1960

In the declining days of summer, long ago, when late August slips seamlessly into early September, a half dozen of the guys I chummed with in high school made the decision to ride the train south to a location close to where the railway line crosses over the Limestone River on a creaky wooden trestle bridge, just upstream from the roar of the Nelson River, as its waters tumbled wildly over the Limestone Rapids. Our destination was a place known by the Canadian National Railway as Mile 352.

Mile posting, a system used two thousand years ago by the Romans, is still used to give a location, and estimate distance on railway lines and on long remote highways. For us, Mile 352, our destination on the Hudson Bay Railway line, is exactly 352 miles by rail from Mile 0, located in The Pas. Mile 352 is also where a small collection of homes, called "section houses," were constructed in the 1920s. It was there that the CNR section hands and their families lived in splendid isolation in a collection of homes in the middle of nowhere, simply a tiny dot on the map, a tiny dot described on that map as the hamlet of Amery.

For those of you unfamiliar with the geography of Manitoba, find a decent map of the province. Tourism Manitoba provides, for free, an excellent highway map that will serve you well. On the map, locate The Pas. Then follow the railway line as it navigates steadily in a lonely northeast direction. But then, just south of Amery, it suddenly veers north, heading toward Churchill. The peculiarity of this abrupt change in route is puzzling until one learns the complicated history of the railway, of Port Nelson on the estuary of the Nelson River, and of the Port of Churchill in the early years of the twentieth century.

The original intent of planners was to construct a port called Port Nelson on the estuary of the Nelson River. Work on this project commenced in 1914 before the outbreak of World War I and continued even while the war was raging in the trenches of France. Why? One would think that the war effort would halt port construction. At this moment in Manitoba's history, the province and the city of Winnipeg had been booming. Up to 1914, thousands of immigrants had arrived, including British and Americans and, from the Russian Empire, Ukrainians, Jews, and German Mennonites. Icelanders fleeing volcanic destruction at home all flooded in, a tidal wave of humanity creating a human mosaic, most settling in English, Ukrainian, Jewish, Icelandic, or Mennonite communities. And incredible as this may sound today, Winnipeg was the newest, wealthiest, and fastest-growing city in North America. And nobody could see any reason why this should change.

Manitoba, it was believed, needed its own deep-water seaport on Hudson Bay, a route by sea to Europe and the markets of the world, a route to export the products of the province and the west, wheat from the farms, ores and precious resources that were sure to be found lying deep within the Precambrian rock exposed thousands of years before by the southern movement of glaciers. That deep water port was to be Port Nelson, a port capable of exporting these resources and,-also in the process, happily generating millions of dollars to be distributed amongst the wealthy grain barons and entrepreneurs living in their mansions in Winnipeg's very expensive Crescentwood and Wellington Crescent neighbourhoods.

Consequently, the government of Canada, spurred on by those wealthy, enthusiastic captains of commerce, spent a fortune building a port and infrastructure to support this port. An artificial island appeared in the estuary, which was then connected to the mainland by a seventeen-span steel truss bridge, designed and prefabricated in Montreal by Dominion Bridge. Rail lines, locomotives, and rolling stock were delivered by sea before the railbed and line were completed. Docks rose on the island, and a brand-new Montreal-built dredge was deployed, a dredge christened "Port Nelson." Work on the port continued throughout the war, but then in 1918, the order suddenly came in to close the operation. The time had come, the order said, to abandon everything. Engineers had been reporting that silting, a natural phenomenon in river estuaries, was an unforeseen problem. The dredge simply could not keep up. The harbour needed constant attention. To add to the port's problems, there was only about an hour and a bit to get a freighter in or out of the port at high tide. This proved to be fatal to the harbour and its future. There is little more to add. Its venture as a deep-water port was ill-starred, and an incredible waste of taxpayers' money. The incompetence demonstrated was unforgiveable. It was clearly breathtaking, and then it was never mentioned again. It was forgotten.

Thus, the abandoned rail line from The Pas lay dormant until 1927 when, once again, the federal government decided to make yet another stab at port creation on Hudson Bay. The rail line now turned to a new choice: north to Churchill where, in 1929 and 1930, a new port, docks, a railhead, and an elevator were built. As for Port Nelson, it was quietly and conveniently left as a historical postscript to an extraordinary failure, a project that most Canadians have no idea existed. And as for that dredge, reputed at the time to be the world's largest, she was mothballed. Then, because of a violent storm in 1924, she was driven ashore to straddle, like a giant beached whale, the docks of Port Nelson—her back broken in two.

As for we boys in the late summer of 1960, we were largely indifferent to our history. We then knew little and cared less about the ghosts of the men who laboured on that line, the ghosts of armies of navvies who collectively built an improbable railway through mosquito-infested swamps and bush, and over roaring, powerful rivers. We thought and cared little for their courage and achievements. Instead, we put our collective heads together, confidently estimating, as only sixteen-year-olds can, what we should take to sustain our needs for a week, keeping in mind we were miles from home, miles from the nearest store, miles from our mothers who would make helpful suggestions. But we, then being sixteen, most certainly knew everything.

The necessities of life thought important by a sixteen- or seventeen-year-old, when compared to helpful suggestions that might be offered by our mothers, were a contest of opposites. A balanced diet was rejected in favour of foods that we could cook quickly and then stuff into our faces to quell the gnawing pangs of hunger. Necessities for us boys meant a couple of cans of loose tobacco and rolling papers, matches, canned baked beans, two or three bags of potatoes, bacon, lard, canned ham or corned beef, peanuts, a couple of bottles of Canadian whisky hidden in a duffle bag, assorted hard candies, flour, baking powder, powdered milk, coffee, tea, a bag of Manitoba brown sugar, and a two-pound tin of strawberry jam—all of this plus sharp knives, a Coleman lantern and spare mantles and fuel for the lantern, cooking utensils, cups, plates, fishing rods and lures, line and hooks, pliers, an axe, playing cards, a couple of .22s plus ammunition, and perhaps a camera or two with rolls of spare black-and-white film to record, for posterity, our adventures.

Our mothers, of course, lamented the lack of healthy food. There was not a hint of fresh fruit, unless you considered strawberry jam fruit. And were baked beans and potatoes vegetables? Who knew? Nutrition and healthy diets were in the domain of our mothers, not ours. We cared little what we ate, just as long as we ate something filling. In our estimation, quantity overruled quality. Give a sixteen-year-old boy the choice between a burger and fries or a large mixed green salad with croutons, and I believe I know what he would choose.

To further augment our fresh-food supply and balance our question-able diet, we made extravagant plans to "live off the land," much like those unnamed heroic characters who inhabited the pages of our history books: the Métis, the Coureurs des Bois, the Nor'Westers, the North-West Mounted Police, or the men of the Hudson's Bay Company. There were, we told our-selves, waters teeming with fish patiently waiting to be caught on our hooks and then fried over an open fire; rabbits that would hop around and then conveniently stop and pose, waiting to be spotted and dispatched with a shot from a trusty .22; or a free produce department of plants that nature would provide, waiting to be picked and enjoyed. Of these, we discovered that only the fish could be counted on. The bunnies, fortunately for them, never appeared to leave their burrows to forage for food and then conveniently stop and pose. And as for the free supply of edible plants, it appeared that nobody wanted to be the king's official food taster and perhaps die from the toxic effect of eating what could be or possibly not be a mushroom. Who knew the difference between a toadstool and a mushroom anyway? And if someone claimed to know, who would believe him? Would he be the first to eat it while we sat around and watched, waiting to see if he died? After all, toadstools and mushrooms looked eerily similar, didn't they?

Our parents deposited us and our gear at the station, with lots of time to catch the evening Churchill-to-Winnipeg-bound train. Much as we appreci-ated them taking us, the last thing we wanted was to have them hanging around until we boarded the day car and waved goodbye. Having them there, waiting. And for what? Today, I would give my most prized possession just to be with my parents, for just a little while. But then, as a self-obsessed youth, it was hugely embarrassing. And to my dismay, Mum and Dad waited on the platform while we boarded the day car and claimed a seat. The car was crowded with the spectrum of passengers found on that train. There were those journeying all the way to Winnipeg who simply refused to pay the extra for a sleeper car accommodation, preferring instead to ride out the journey in seats that partially reclined. And there were others, like us, riding to little-known stops in the middle of nowhere. The thing to understand about that train and those passengers in the mid-twentieth century was that the train was a lifeline, a sort of super bus to be boarded and exited as required by those who lived along the tracks. Thus, the Saturday evening train was crowded with folks, many of whom had come to town catching the train by stopping it at lonely spots along the track, by request, and then boarding it and presumably paying the conductor the fare. When the train arrived in Churchill at around eight o'clock in the morning, if all went well and there were no freight trains nor derailments to deal with, they conducted their business in town. They shopped, buying the kids new boots or jeans or underwear, stocking up on groceries or buying supplies, and, for some, having completed their business, saying a lengthy hello to the bartenders at either the Churchill or Hudson Hotels. Later, in a jolly state, they would then say a reluctant goodbye and reclaim their seats on the evening train. Most of the folks who were going to overnight on the train all the way to Winnipeg had, upon boarding the sleeper cars, made their way to their seats, which, by railway illusion, like a magician for the railway, would change two seats into comfortable bunks—an upper and a lower—an hour or two after the train departed Churchill. That magician was, of course, a helpful, courteous, and often black porter.

I recall finding a seat, making myself comfortable, and then looking down the still-busy station platform. Still faithful, my parents stood there until the train, with a succession of quick jerks that then transitioned into smooth motion, began its long, lonely haul south. My Dad, in the typical way he had, gave a couple of nods, and then turned to leave. Mother, though, who wore her scarf on her head as she was wont, gave a sort of sideways wave. She then became a figure blending with those still on the platform and disappeared from view. She had worn her headscarf from her days in Word War II, when factory-working girls took scarves from a safety item to a fashion item. She never stopped wearing one. She, like the Queen, often wore one. Mother was rarely a hat kind of girl.

With the rhythm of wheels rolling beneath our feet, we settled down in our seats, aware that we were on the edge of an adventure—perhaps, up to that moment, the singular most important adventure of our young lives. After all, there we were, on a train, just sixteen or seventeen years old, heading for a place we had never before been, to arrive in the dark at midnight, with no mother fussing. We were leaving the comforts of home and the security and benefits that home brings, and we were determined not just to survive but, indeed, prosper on our own. In our minds, we were like countless millions of other teenagers plunging into the unknown, whether running away off to fight in a war or, like us, experiencing something we had never done alone for the very first time, something new, flavoured with perhaps the slightest suggestion of danger. That, to a sixteen -or seventeen-year-old, was indeed intoxicating.

Around midnight, in total darkness as it was now late August and the earth was fast slipping into the northern hemisphere's autumnal mode, the train slowly squealed to a halt at Mile 352. We had arrived at Amery and were as excited as if we were in New York City for the first time.

We were ushered out of the car by the conductor, and just as Neil Armstrong's foot touched the surface of the lunar unknown a few years later, our feet also touched the unknown of the gravel railbed, deep in the isolation of the Canadian wilderness. We carefully made our way in the darkness, along the spill of loose stones leaking from between the rail ties, toward the yellow pool of light cast by the baggage car to claim—and pull to one side in a pile—our food, tent, and kit bags. Then the door of the freight car rolled closed with a thud, and we stood submerged in a void of almost total darkness. The train, with a series of jerks and squeals, once again began its slow and steady roll south until, in smooth and constant motion, it disappeared into the black velvet of the night. The sound of the wheels on steel gradually decreased, then was lost in the clamour of fast-running water. As my eyes adjusted, in the cool night air of that early morning in August, I immediately felt an encompassing, overwhelming primeval embrace. Simultaneously, I was terrified yet thrilled. We had arrived! Now, the first real adventure of our young lives had begun.

ROLLING, ROLLING, ROLLING
DOWN THE RIVER

By the hissing light of our Coleman lantern, and by a combination of limited skills we would never admit to, and lots of luck we would also never admit to, the tent was unrolled and then erected in a clearing close to the railway tracks. The food and equipment were covered, in case of rain, with a tarp held down with rocks. Our sleeping bags were then arranged near each other within the tent, and upon crawling wearily into them, we fell gratefully into a deep, much needed sleep, lulled by the nearby chorus of fast-moving water.

Then, for the next six days, for almost a glorious week, we fished the waters of those northern rivers. The Limestone, a tributary of the Nelson River, was close by, not too far from our campsite. It was the Limestone we heard running in the quiet of night, a sound augmented by the distant roar of the Limestone Rapids. Each day, down the banks of the Limestone, with rods held high and tackleboxes swinging, we scrabbled and stood at the very edge in the grass and cast our lines into the fast-flowing stream. It was deep in places, but we soon discovered some shallows over which we could cross by foot to the southern bank, being careful not to slip. The water rose to mid-calf, and initially we took great care in crossing. But again, with the bound-less bravado of youth, and having the security of previous crossings with no incident, we grew increasingly overconfident, without falling in and possibly being swept away, lucky for us. Such is the invincibility of the young. There was a nearby trestle bridge crossing the river and the question arises, why didn't we bother using that bridge? The journey across that bridge and along the south bank of the Limestone to the same place we could reach by fording the river took around thirty minutes as compared to five minutes. So why bother? And we didn't. Being sixteen or seventeen, swimming in a lake of hormones made us immortal, as it would time and time again in the months and years to follow. In our youth, like most young men, we were inherently lazy, fearless, and impetuous and immortal. A dangerous combination.

We fished and caught whitefish and pike, commonly referred to as "jack-fish." The whitefish was delicious, the pike, full of bones and, often, partially digested frogs, ducklings, or goslings. So, it was discarded. We ate fish every day—fried, boiled, baked, fried again. Fish with potatoes also fried, boiled, baked, and fried again, formed the basis of a monotonous but relatively healthy diet for an active young man. To alter the monotony of our meals, we would heat cans of baked beans and mix them with the flesh of potatoes baked in a fire. And we ate everything, even the partially scorched skins of the potatoes. We were young and hungry and never gained weight, no matter what we stuffed into our bodies.

I recall that on those warm, sunny days, we'd walk the banks of the Limestone and then, with growing confidence, the west bank of the Nelson. The Limestone, in comparison to the Nelson, was a mere tributary. In its own right, it might have been a river of note, but compared to the Nelson, into which its waters emptied, it was as a raindrop descending a windowpane.

On those August afternoons, after fording the Limestone to its southern bank, we happily fished and chatted for hours, occasionally moving to a location that perhaps was more promising. There was a small island, a placid spot near the mouth of the Limestone where sediment carried downstream was deposited in the quieter waters. The island was achieved easily by wading over some shallows. It was here we discovered a net stretched across the water on the other side of the small island. Although I acknowledge that net fishing is not a sport, it is a necessity for some. We concluded that the net belonged to the fellows who worked as section hands for the CNR and were living in the section houses in Amery. But this conclusion was wrong, as we were shortly to discover.

These shallows to the island were perfect for washing ourselves, and we certainly needed a place like that. We'd strip down and run into the calf-deep water. Standing semi-naked in the shallows, we threw water at each other, shrieking and hollering at the top of our lungs, scaring off any bears within a three-mile radius, and having the time of our lives. My God, life was wonderful!

The distance from the mouth of the Limestone River to the rapids on the Nelson was relatively short and potentially hazardous. Care had to be taken. Near the joining of the two rivers, the Limestone appeared to move faster, and the roar of the Limestone Rapids filled the air in increasing volume as we approached. Here, a simple misstep, slip, or accidental turn of the ankle could possibly cast one into the river and on into its turmoil.

The rapids were immense. Stone and thrashing water from shore to shore joined and then parted as if in a choreographed dance. Rocky barriers held back charging walls of water, pulled by the constant force of gravity down steep, stony inclines, falling, and throwing spray high into the air, which then fell back to join the crashing, cascading swirls, and whirlpools farther down.

The air, saturated with spray, made staying dry all but impossible and made one aware as to where to put one's foot for fear of misstepping on the wet, slippery surface, a misstep that could potentially be catastrophic. But being sixteen or seventeen, we confidently buried that fear, as we knew with utmost certainty, we would never be a statistic. We were, after all, like the gods in the pantheon: immortal.

On one occasion, we spotted a distant helicopter hovering, then moving back and forth around and over the rapids. We had no idea what was going on and concluded that it was probably a machine hired by—what else in our imaginations? —rich Americans who wanted a bird's-eye view of the waters below, perhaps looking for places to drop a line and catch the trophy fish. Realistically, we had no answers, but conjecture is fun. However, conjecture lacks facts and is usually wrong.

The tragic truth, I believe, is that we were watching the beginning of the end of the rapids. Man, in his quest to prove he can master whatever he sets his mind to, was planning to master these rapids, just as he had mastered other sets of rapids farther upstream. After we had camped and fished at 352 on two annual occasions and had then abandoned our fishing expeditions to go to university, the rapids were destroyed by the building of a giant coffer dam and then a massive hydroelectric plant, named, with great irony, "Sundance."

The rush for power in the south again trumped nature in the north. I carry a sense of overwhelming privilege blended with a deep sense of sorrow that my friends and I were among the very last to see the great rapids alive, although at the time, I had no premonition of what was to happen. Not knowing is sometimes best. Enough said!

Have you ever been fortunate enough to meet a person who, in some way, gave your life a new compass bearing? I have. The day I first met Judah was one of these days, a day I'll remember for the rest of my life. And incredible as it may sound, that day centred on, of all things, potatoes, and fish.

We had been fishing, hopefully casting our lines and lures into the Limestone, and, in the late afternoon, returned to camp, happy and hungry, looking forward to a fish fry. We had caught a couple of large whitefish that promised to be exactly what the chef ordered: pan-fried whitefish with boiled potatoes. Predictable, honest fare. Especially when prepared on an ancient wood-fuelled stove, which we had found in a nearby bush, that produced either a meal or, if one was not careful, a cremation. To avoid one person taking all the glory, or the blame, for the food that appeared on our plates, we rotated being the cook and discovered, not surprisingly, that some of us knew how to cook and others didn't. Regardless of the quality of the cooking, we ate almost everything that landed on our plates.

I cannot recall who was responsible, but the cook of the day discovered, after rummaging around inside of the tent, that several of our potatoes had disappeared only to be miraculously replaced by four large whitefish. It certainly was not a biblical miracle. It was, instead, clearly a case of someone deciding, "You've got what I want, and I've got what you want, and as you're currently not here, let's trade anyway."

The answer to this conundrum of the fish and missing potatoes we solved that evening, as we sat around the campfire rolling, quite industriously, our quota of rollie cigarettes that we would smoke the next day. A tall First Nations gentleman crossed the tracks and made his way toward our fire. He then spoke in that singularly musical style that many Indigenous persons, for whom English is a second language, use when speaking English. We were, to be honest, somewhat taken aback when he appeared. We offered him a cigarette that he took with a smile. Then, by a combination of smiles, hand gestures, and that musical English, he made it clear that he was the culprit, the person responsible for the fish-and-potato mystery. This was our introduction to Judah, a warm, generous man who apparently lived in Shamatawa, an isolated Northern Manitoba community. And while visiting family in Amery, he netted whitefish, four of which landed in our tent. It was, we learned, his net we found just off the island. He, unlike we who fished for pleasure, took his fishing seriously. After all, food was food, and the net represented a serious attempt at fishing.

He then surprised us with an offer we could not refuse: a day trip the next day, canoeing a few kilometres down the Nelson, downstream from the Limestone Rapids. Little did we know at the time that in a few years, this would be impossible because of the dam construction. The Limestone Rapids that we heard roaring as we fell asleep in the deep of a boreal night would be gone within a decade, under thousands of tons of concrete and an artificial lake. But now is now, and then was then. And then, there was a wild, untamed river on that part of the Nelson. We eagerly accepted Judah's offer to travel even a small portion of the great river.

The next morning found us in the canoe, moving downstream with the current, the water beneath us flowing steadily, consistently toward Hudson Bay, in the basking warmth of a late August day. (The current steadily flows toward Hudson Bay even in the bitter cold of winter, moving under the ice.) We happily cast our lines and fished. And while in the canoe, we neglected the basic rule of boating: we wore no life vests. And Judah apparently didn't believe in them either, as he had none in his canoe and did not wear one himself. This was, of course, a time of vastly different values, when ordinary folks did not use seat belts in cars, heavily salted their food, allowed six-year-olds to lie in the rear window shelf of fast-moving sedans, smoked like chimneys, and used asbestos in brakes, insulation, and ceiling tiles. So, the failure to wear or possess life vests was not unusual.

We happily fished and caught both whitefish and jackfish. Jackfish, in the freshwater marine world, must be the T. Rexes of their watery domain. They are aggressive, eat just about anything that moves, and come equipped with a set of teeth that have just one purpose: to seize and hold onto their prey. There is no escape.

I recall that somebody, I cannot recall whom, in a moment of madness, poked at a freshly caught jackfish lying, but still very much alive, in the bottom of the canoe. The jackfish instinctively lunged at the finger, caught it in its mouth, and clamped down. The result was that the finger was trapped by an array of razor-sharp teeth, all pointing inward. To release the finger, we had to cut the mouth to give room to move the finger forward. Finally, out came the finger, worse for wear, but fortunately, it survived. The fish, however, did not.

As we drifted downstream, caught in the current of the great river, we marvelled at its size. At that time, where we were, it was still wild and wonderful and untamed. The river was extraordinarily wide, with high banks that formed steep barriers from the base to the top. And along the banks were stretches of pebbly beaches where a weary canoeist could pull in, sit, rest, and watch. And we did. We pulled into a sunny west-side beach and hauled the canoe ashore, sat, and watched the river steam by, on its way to the Bay and the sea. There, we fried a fish lunch over an open fire. No fine-dining restaurant in London, Paris, or New York could equal this, a meal eaten without pretention or, indeed, good manners. And to think, we enjoyed a lunch that, a couple of hours earlier, had been a fish swimming in the cold depths of the river, also looking for something to eat. It saw the lure, lunged at it, and was, as they say, well and truly hooked. You can't get any fresher than that!

And one more point I must here emphasize. Judah has been locked deep within my memory ever since. His generosity, his sense of humour, and his acceptance have remained with me. He delighted in our pleasure. And although we met but briefly, his kindness toward us was one of the great influences of my life. And all of this because of a trade of potatoes for fish.

The six days flew by. Friday was our last day, and we spent the morning fishing and the afternoon taking down the camp, packing our gear, tarp, and tent, and hoping it wouldn't rain. It didn't!

To amuse ourselves, we threw a couple of cans of baked beans into the fire just to watch them explode and then visited Mr. Beardy, the section foreman, in his section house. Mrs. Beardy, a jovial soul who apparently liked company, insisted we have tea, while carefully inspecting the cups and wiping each one vigorously with the hem of her "pinny."

As we drank Mrs. Beardy's tea, enjoying her hospitality, Mr. Beardy assured us the train would stop at Amery on its way north and, if on time, would arrive in the early hours of Saturday morning. So, we had a waiting game to play. And, to top it off, by around 9:00 p.m., the sun would set, and within the hour, our world would be in the deep dark of the bush. All we had to do—besides beat off the irritation of mosquitoes that seemed capable of feasting not only on exposed skin but also on parts covered—was wait on the tracks in anticipation of a train heading north, heading home to Churchill.

By half past eight, we watched the sun begin to set. In the half-light, we built a fire. And then, in the flickering light, idle talk and questions flew like sparks from the spitting logs in the late evening air. Our concerns were magnified with the coming of night. Darkness always does this. We sat, a small group, encircling the fire, staring at the dots of darting sparks. Then, by half past nine, nothing but the ink black sky with the bright constellation of stars. Reluctantly, we watched the fire slowly sink into a glowing cauldron of embers.

Then, softly, riding above the sound of running water, the slightest hint of a new sound in the distance, a subtle note hanging on the early morning air, drifting through the cover of darkness.

"Can you hear something?"

"Yeah, yeah. Yeah! I can!"

A sound hardly heard initially over the rush of the waters of the Limestone but a sound, nevertheless. A simple vibration pushed through the chill of the morning air. Then, a deeper note, growing slowly, growing into a chorus of notes, building one upon the other. A chorus of notes cascading into a single, throbbing sound of a big diesel locomotive.

Floating like an apparition, bobbing over the trees, a light danced, keeping pace with the sound, which, as if on cue, changed tone as steel wheels on steel rails encountered the bridge over the river. Out of the cloak of night came the very different rumble of wheels rolling on rails set upon a wooden span.

Gradually, the pulsing sound of a big diesel engine grew louder, a sound led by the locomotive's bright beam of light cutting through the dark late summer air. Clearly, audibly, the engine and procession of railcars slowed and then stopped with a squeal of brakes, close to where we stood. Realizing that time was important, we hurriedly gathered our tent and kit bags and carried them toward the yellow lit door of the waiting baggage car, where we hoisted them into the safekeeping of a man whose outline stood in the dimly lit opening. The door then closed with a thud, and we were once again left standing in the dark.

As our eyes adjusted, we made our way forward, toward a conductor with a flashlight who stood in the pale-yellow pool of light that marked our car, following the uneven gravel that had spilled from the railbed. Wearily, we climbed the step into the dimly lit interior. It was half full, carrying passengers, many of whom, like us, had been picked up along the track and were heading into town. Some were sleeping or trying to sleep. A few kids lay sprawled across two seats, sleeping soundly, head on one seat, tail on the other. Finding some seats vacant, we settled contentedly into the luxury of the comfort of a CN Day coach recliner, where I promptly fell into a deep and, I believe, dreamless sleep. I was tired. Dog tired. More tired than I could ever recall. Too tired to even dream. I was awakened by the jarring cry of the conductor calling out, "Churchill! Next stop, last stop! Churchill, folks! Up and at 'em. Churchill!"

I peered through the window with half-open eyes still scrunched from sleep and saw cars moving along the highway. The familiar world, my small corner of the world, my hometown, came into view, accompanied by a series of banging jolts as the engineer applied the brakes. Gradually, the train slowed and then finally slid to a grudging halt alongside the platform of the station.

I was home! And there on the platform, as expected, just to reassure themselves I was in one piece and not overly punctured from fishing hooks, stood my parents. Dad, upon seeing me, would nod in that restrained English way he had, and I knew that my mother would fuss. In truth, I quite liked being fussed over. But only in the privacy of home. And never in front of my friends, who I know shared similar fears about their mothers.

My journey to Mile 352 and the great river was over. But then, in the early '60s, my life's journey was just beginning, although at the time I did not realize it. That trip put me firmly on a path, one of many I could choose from, a path that would carry me through the multitude of experiences and choices we call life.

I have been on those paths for seven decades now, paths that began long ago, in a wondrous land, on a sunny August day, on that magical river, with my friends and that man from Shamatawa. I couldn't ask for a better beginning, could I?

SUMMER VACATION 2—THE
UNIVERSITY YEARS, 1964–1968
COME FLY WITH ME

Unlike many of the guys I chummed with who lived in the Churchill townsite, once high school was done and dusted, Wayne and I made the life-changing decision not to work locally as labourers or truck drivers but to continue with our education and attend a university in the distant south, more than 1,200 kilometres away. For many of our friends, the siren call of certain well-paid employment in return for only partial secondary schooling proved far too attractive to resist. School often played second fiddle to the allure of easy money. Thus, one by one, slowly, slowly they drifted from a high school they found irrelevant and worked for various employers that, at the time, needed strong backs to labour on the docks, on the dams under construction on the Nelson River, or for the company building the new, super long runway at Fort Churchill for the USAF's Strategic Air Command.

"Hey man," they'd say to us, waving wads of cash and poking us in the shoulders with that air of youthful certainty.

"What the hell you still at school for? Hell, man. You know . . ." and here you may insert the name of any employer competing for labour at that time in Churchill, so let's call one of them "ZEDCO."

"You know ZEDCO's paying two dollars and fifty cents an hour. Who cares about school?"

Yes, the world was indeed their oyster. But not mine. Why not? Well, to start with, my dad cared. Oysters or not. And because he cared, so did I. The old man was a steady guiding light in my life. Our relationship, like many of my friends' father–son relationships, was often strained and bruised from hitting life's bumps. But I respected him and valued his opinions. He was a source of working man's wisdom, and I listened.

"Only donkeys work," he'd philosophize. "Don't be a bloody donkey. They're nothing but asses anyway."

In some strange way, the old man seemed to believe that only manual workers actually worked. People in offices didn't. At least not in the same way. They just sat at their desks, lifting, and moving bits of paper. The heaviest thing they lifted was a pen. And after all, didn't office workers, unlike him, leave the office at five o'clock with the same spotlessly clean shirts and clean hands they had arrived with at eight that morning? Dad came home covered with the evidence of hard work. In his mind, he worked, and they didn't. He was determined that his sons would, come hell or high water, have clean hands and spotless shirts come "punching out time," as he put it. Also, in a moment of unexpected generosity, the old man was prepared to pay a portion of my first year at university. In fact, his portion was substantial, as I only had July and August to earn enough to pay for, perhaps, 40 percent of my tuition, room and board, transportation back and forth—twice—and perhaps fifteen dollars a week spending money. The rest came from him, for one year only. After that, he hinted, I was on my own, paying my own way, though occasionally, when I was stretching my dollars at school, with another two or three months to go, a letter with a couple of twenty-dollar bills in the envelope would appear, in Dad's handwriting, but always from Mum and then Dad. To ensure I did not fritter away any of the summer earnings "renting beer," as he put it, in the local Churchill or Hudson Hotels, he happily organized an additional evening job for me, working for ninety cents an hour at the Garrison Theatre, from 6:00 p.m. to 10:30 p.m., for six evenings out of seven. The theatre was closed every Thursday. This job I kept for three summers, and it certainly accomplished two things. It put the brakes on my supporting the breweries and, consequently, put extra into my bank. And another plus with the job in the theatre was that I got to see the movies for free from the incredibly hot and noisy projectionist's room. It was from this room that the projectionist, a kindly fellow with infinite patience and a hearty sense of humour, between reels, would show me how to load and rewind the projectors. Or we would look out over the audience at the shenanigans that went on below, "down there." No more needs to be said, except, I must say, I was amazed at the agility of some couples.

Come September, both Wayne and I packed our bags and set off on our grand adventure in the south, 1,200 kilometres from home and our parents, making new friends and, in Wayne's case, meeting a lovely girl and marrying in 1965. They were together until Wayne's untimely passing.

For me, the day came to depart Churchill by train in early September for school in the south. Dad took me to the station in his '57 Ford Ranchero, a car that only sat two comfortably. Mother stayed home, which was for the better, as she could be an emotional girl who wore her heart and colours on her sleeve. At the station, my case was checked through to Winnipeg, and the old man, keeping himself busy, found my car, a sleeper with an upper bunk that was reserved for me. He ushered me onto the steps of the car, gave me a restrained sort of man hug, and then retreated for his Ranchero. He then sat there, as I could plainly see from my seat on the train, probably to make sure I didn't make a run for it and escape. Only when the train began to move out of the station did he back out and head for the highway and, I presumed, home.

I watched Dad's car pick up speed as the train moved at a progressively increased but still slow tempo and then saw his car disappear behind the squat outline of HMCS Churchill and the buildings of Camp 20, the Inuit settlement.

As I sat, I watched the familiar background scenery pass by, scenery I had haunted as I grew up, wandering up and down the tracks with my trusty .22 in hand, scenery as familiar as the back of the proverbial hand. I had to admit, viewing it from the comfort of a CN sleeper car gave me a different perspective on the passing scene. I then realized the road crossing at Goose Creek was fast approaching, and I was curious to see it again, from the view of a passing train and not waiting patiently for the train to pass, as was my usual wont. Yes, there it was, and to my utter amazement, there was the old man, waiting all alone, at the crossing, sitting in his '57 Ford Ranchero. The headlights of the car flashed on and off as my railcar passed, and then in a blink, Dad was gone. And, for the very first time in my life, I felt absolutely alone, almost fragile, apprehensive about the tomorrows yet to come. I now had to become an adult in an adult world, a world I feared yet yearned for.

And I knew one other thing. Despite his overreactions, the old man used denial as a shield to hide his real feelings. He hid his emotions well, but occasionally, he dropped his guard. This was one such moment.

Thus, the first year of university flew by. Kennedy was killed. The Beatles arrived. Skirts began to shrink. And by March, with the world in a state of transition, I had two firm offers of full-time summer employment at home in Churchill. One was from my old standby, the Royal Canadian Engineers, and the other from Pan American World Airways, the American company contracted to operate the American launch facility operating a few kilometres from Fort Churchill. Both offered the same rate of pay for similar job descriptions. Previously, I had worked each summer for the Engineers and felt a nostalgic pull of loyalty toward them, but the opposing pull of working in a different place for a different employer was strong. "Change," as the old saying goes, "is as good as a rest." Not that I needed a rest. I needed money and, unlike the Engineers, Pan Am had a reputation for paying overtime at one and a half times the rate of regular pay. That kind of change was the kind of change I needed to deposit into my bank account. Thus, because of the money, I opted for Pan Am. Pan American, an airline that flew worldwide until the destruction of a Boeing 747 by terrorists over Lockerbie, Scotland in the 1990s, seemed to have an eerie connection with the US government and had a knack for being in line when contracts were handed out. The role of Pan Am in Churchill was to operate the launch facility for NASA, the United States Air Force, the US Army, and, last but not least, the National Research Council of Canada. What Pan Am, a private airline, was doing launching sounding rockets and conducting secret space research was a topic of gossip and constant conversation in Churchill. It did seem strange. The presence of the US military and of Pan Am, like most things American, was "in your face" and brash, and with a strange sense of absolute certainty that they and God were on the right side of the fence, and the heathen Soviets were on the other. American Army and Air Force officers, sleek in brass-buttoned uniforms, visited the warehouse where I worked and had, as we could see, long and sometimes agitated conversations with the very American Pan Am manager in his office. Mysterious boxes appeared from launch with directions to send them to Edwards Air Force Base, which I later discovered was key to the American Apollo space program. What was in those boxes that came and went, I never knew, and I knew enough to never ask. Those boxes were often shipped in and out posthaste via US military aircraft—the US Military Air Transport Service—aircraft flown by Air Force pilots, 90 percent of whom were generally young, good-natured, boyishly handsome, and polite. Pilots who looked and behaved just like those boyish Hollywood small-town boys we watched on the silver screen on Friday evenings. But there were a few, as is true everywhere, who were officious and full of their own self-importance. Often, quietly muttered side remarks, like those whispered asides in a Shakespearean play, could be softly heard from us as the officious arsehole left the aircraft and disappeared down the steps. Middle fingers were a common salute.

The one big difference I discovered about Pan Am, when compared to working for the Canadian Civil Service, was the fact that Pan Am was not unionized. Being a working-class kid with working-class values brought up in a strongly working-class, pro-union home, I immediately noticed the differences in attitudes between Pan Am and the Canadian Civil Service. Pan Am employees, although well paid, appeared to have no recourse to appeal if let go. On the other hand, releasing a civil service member—let's say from my old man's plumbing shop—would entail meetings with the shop's stewards, the foreman, the employee, and the company sergeant major; more talks with the union; lots of paper shuffling; and once, even a trip for Dad to Winnipeg in his capacity as foreman, and all often for naught, or a slap on the wrist, a reprimand in writing, which was then placed in the employee's file to gather dust and be forgotten. Pan Am's attitude seemed, to my novice understanding, to be quick and ruthless, quite American, an "every man for himself" attitude, a meaner, less kind sort of philosophy. It was swift, efficient, and final. And that was that! Hands were dusted and replacements appointed.

The warehouse, where I was employed, was enormous, one of three built into the rock itself. There was an inner tunnel with loading docks for trucks and an exterior railhead built adjacent to outer docks, where cargo could be unloaded and then dollied into the building.

The warehouse stored most of everything that a large complex needed, from furniture to carpets, to vacuums to clean those carpets, to beds and mattresses, and even to automobile and truck engines stored in round containers, stored in oil to protect them. Everything was "part-numbered" and stacked on shelving that rose three metres high. To reach a requested product, a forklift with a wooden pallet lifted somebody standing on the pallet up to the appropriate level, and the product was pulled. Removing the product from the warehouse would identify where the product was sent and could trigger a renewal by the office crew. One of my jobs that summer was to build a couple of safety pallets so that a product could be safely identified and removed without someone falling off. I built them, and they worked!

Requested deliveries from the warehouse to an address were a favourite of ours, especially delivering to a certain PMQ where lived an American officer's pretty, young wife, a girl with straight white teeth, a cute turned-up nose, and hair in the style of the late '50s and early '60s, piled high and sprayed stiff, resembling a beehive, looking like Sandra Dee, Kim Novak, or Doris Day. She would tell us, as she delicately puffed at her cigarette, where to put the new couch, table and chairs, and bed and mattress.

"Over there, y'all. My, My. Gosh, golly. Isn't that just purrrfect? Thank y'all."

And we would smile politely, ask if there was anything else she wanted, and then leave. Once in the truck, like kids loose in a candy store, we were free to safely comment on her and declare how lucky her husband was.

The management team in the warehouse office were all Americans; the clerical staff, a mix of Americans and Canadians; and the crew that worked the floor, entirely Canadian. Relations between the Canadians and Americans were cordial, although there was, just beneath the surface, a streak of anti-American resentment among the Canadians. One scratch on the surface could bring those feelings bubbling up. And never, from my brief experience, did the two groups socialize outside the worksite.

The warehouse manager, who was unmistakeably a New Yorker with that obvious New York City accent and attitude, was a short balding man with a pleasant disposition. To me, he resembled a children's toy that boasted how he wobbled but would never fall down. He was almost as wide as he was tall. I liked him, despite the fact that he was an American, a fact that I had also forgiven my first Southern belle girlfriend for. Most of the other Americans seemed to originate from the Confederacy. I recall one very pleasant fellow from a state like South Carolina or Kentucky, and who I found almost impossible to understand, once got really angry with me. He thought that I, as my old man would say, was "taking the mick." One day, you see, this son of the Confederacy called out across the concrete width of an enormous echo chamber of a warehouse.

"John!"

I perked up.

"John, y'all seen annaalcaan?"

He obviously wanted something. But what? I had absolutely no idea.

I responded, "Annaalcaan?" I slavishly mimicked him.

"Yes, annaalcaan. Y'all seen annaalcaan?" By now he was becoming a bit testy.

"What's an annaalcaan?" I was honestly confused.

By now he was agitated, getting angry with me!

"Annaalcaan." he repeated. "Y'all seen one?"

I was equally ticked off. What on earth was an "annaalcaan"? There was a communication gulf between us, between two people who claimed to speak a common tongue—English. I gave in and shrugged; the way Frenchmen do to antagonize *les Anglaise*. He then figured out that I had absolutely no idea what he was saying.

"Fawget it," he said.

Later, he showed me what he'd wanted. Turned out he wanted an oil can. Three words. Yes, some Americans do indeed speak a language that is not really English, a language sometimes just as foreign to me as Russian or Chinese.

An obvious question at this point is: Why were the Americans so busy piling millions of dollars into a remote launch facility on the edge of Hudson Bay? What did they want? What were they up to? Like most things the Americans do, self-interest always trumps anything else. Well, first of all, I must tell you that nobody told me, so all I can rely on was the little I gleaned from local gossip and educated guesses. The first thing you should know was that Churchill's rocket launchers were busy. There were lots and lots of launches, so many, in fact, that Churchill was reputed to be the world's busiest rocket launch site with more suborbital launches than anywhere else on earth, with rockets like the Black Brant, designed and built in Winnipeg. And not only did rockets soar into space, but there was the occasional helium balloon that slowly ascended, finally resembling a bright new star as it rose to incredible altitudes. We gathered from the talk around town that the objective of these remarkable research rockets was to reach a suborbital altitude of close to 1,000 kilometres, where the aurora borealis, more commonly known as the Northern Lights, danced, and twirled across the heavens in a heavenly ballroom called the Van Allen belt. Why the Americans were so interested in the Northern Lights, I can't say for sure. Things of natural beauty they may be, but this is not what drew the American military complex into investigating them. The military mind is far more practical. The Northern Lights were a problem to be solved, not natural phenomena of mysterious beauty. We, who lived in the North, did know that the appearance of the aurora interfered with and completely swallowed radio communication. Local talk marvelled at the enormous piles of cash the United States' military minds were willing to throw at research into the aurora and conjectured the Americans were attempting to find a solution to the radio communication problem. And it was not so that my friends and I could happily listen to crystal clear southern radio stations broadcasting in a frequency that would blast through the Northern Lights conundrum. But, and again this is what the local rumour mill was saying, the Americans were there to solve the erratic radio communication problem they were having. True or not, I cannot say. Local folklore suggested that the Americans were certainly up to something important and were being footloose and free with their dollars, that's for sure. But nobody told us why. It was their secret. And it remained their secret.

One parting thought. Every summer with the shipping season, along with the assortment of floating Greek rust buckets, scruffy British ships, or the neat-as-a-pin Norwegian freighters, came the inevitable Soviet freighters, looking more like floating radar stations than simple tramp freighters. Like flies to honey, they came with mysterious domes and whirling antennae. They certainly had a purpose beyond carrying Canadian wheat, and certainly discouraged visiting nosy locals once tied to dockside. The Russians, too, seemed curious about American activity in that remote corner of the world.

The highlight or, I really do believe, the lowlight of my four and a half months of employment with Pan Am occurred about a month prior to my leaving, when I was once again to catch the slow train south to attend class. This was, you must understand, completely unplanned and unintended, a moment when the fates, for some reason, were unhappy with me, a time when my planets and stars and other celestial bits and bobs were not aligned. It was an event that was to haunt me like a full ten-year prison sentence without parole.

Several sturdy crates had arrived in the warehouse, standing about a metre and a quarter high, all made of sturdy pine, and all nailed together so that each could survive the long, bumpy ride from Somewhere, USA, to Churchill Research Range, Manitoba, Canada. I was told to open the boxes to reveal their contents.

One by one, the nails holding the boxes together surrendered to the bite of the puller, but one did not. I again placed the nail puller over the nail head, slammed the ring down to bite on the nail, and pulled.

I woke up in hospital. The pain was as if Sonny Liston had subjected my face to ten rounds of pounding. I could barely see. All I remembered was pulling the length of the puller toward me. That was it! By chance, the puller had slipped off the nail head and the blunt iron end of the tool hit me on the left side of my nose. Luckily, it missed my eye and my forehead! Either of those could have been a far worse consequence. And I still had my teeth. But my beautiful, graceful nose was a mess. I was left to the tender mercies of a young Canadian Army doctor who, after taking X-rays, gently put one hand on my forehead, said, "This won't hurt," and pulled with the other hand at what had been my nose. The pain was unspeakable. He then stuffed some packing up my nostrils and covered my nose with a cloth adhesive bandage. That, my friends, was his attempt at plastic surgery. He gave me a small box of painkillers and sent me off, telling me to take a few days' leave and see him, or another sympathetic army doctor on duty, in a week.

The next day, the skin under the bandage covering my nose began to itch horribly. And the following day, it was worse. It was so bad that I hurried to see a doctor who examined me and then told me that I was allergic to the adhesive bandage. Who knew? I didn't. And neither did Mum or Dad. And this was to be the start of a weird and wonderful family of allergies I was to discover lying in ambush for me as I wandered through life. The doctor's solution was to leave the nose exposed to the air and remove the packing later.

Eventually, healing occurred. After several weeks, the swelling around my eyes disappeared; the technicolour blue, green, and yellow slowly cleared; and my nose was not straight but slightly bent like a punch-drunk boxer's. And

I could not breathe easily through my left nostril. But as with most injuries, we humans adapt, get used to them, and carry on. At least, that is what I did.

Ten years later, in 1972, my registered-nurse, recently wed, quite-pregnant wife, fed up, I think, from my snoring as she attempted to sleep at night, and very much aware I had breathing problems, arranged for me to see a plastic surgeon who practised in the clinic where she worked. He examined my nose and, not to anyone's surprise, diagnosed that my nose was indeed bent and needed to be straightened. That procedure was arranged and completed, free of charge as this was not cosmetic but necessary surgery. But the story does not quite end there.

On the night after the surgery, in hospital, with my nose encased in a plaster cast and my nostrils completely plugged with cotton, making any breathing impossible, I was given a medication and promptly fell asleep, comforted by the knowledge that my wife would be with me when I was discharged in the morning, after the doctor dropped by to see me. As I slept, I dreamed. And in that dream, I saw that I was taking the cast off my nose and then carefully putting the cast onto the side table beside my bed. Then I awoke. I felt for my nose, and it was there. But to my horror, the cast wasn't. It was exactly where my dream said it was—on the side table.

The night nurse was very unhappy, as was the doctor who had to come in to attend me at three o'clock in the morning. He curtly reminded me that I was lucky my nose was not smeared all over my face nor over the pillow. And, yes, the cast was refitted that night and was still there when I was seen by the surgeon the next morning. He was still unhappy with me though.

Living with a cast was a nuisance, especially while wearing glasses. I am not good without my glasses. You see, I am short-sighted in one eye and far-sighted in the other and need my glasses to do almost any task that requires sight. And that, dear friends, involves just about everything. The problem for me, then, was that my glasses refused to stay put while balanced on top of the cast. So as a solution, I took to taping the arms of my glasses to my temple area and tried to avoid moving my head too much. I did get some strange looks from folks, especially in cars that drew up beside ours. I realized that I was definitely a sight with a nose cast and glasses perched on the cast. So, in response to those strange looks, I gave them a regal, House of Windsor–like wave of the wrist. Then the onlookers either waved back or looked straight ahead, frightened, perhaps, that the fellow in the car next to them was a wee bit odd. Upon reflection, maybe they were right.

Now, ten years after introducing my nose to the blunt end of a puller, and thanks to my pregnant wife's efforts and an unhappy plastic surgeon, I could breathe again. And Val, for a while at least, was free from my snoring. As the Bard said, "All's well that ends well." And yes, this did indeed end well. I have been breathing well for the past fifty years. And as for that marriage to the pregnant registered nurse—well, that's still going well too!

AM I BLUE?

For you youngsters, I realize the song "Am I Blue?" reaches back to a day long before many of you were born. But I am sure you would recognize it. Personally, I love Linda Ronstadt's dreamy version. Now what has this song got to do with the topic at hand? The answer is in the title. The colour blue was a dominant colour in my youth. I clearly recall the intense cut blue of a subarctic sky set against the brilliant, unspoiled undulations of blue-tinged snow below; my old man's sky-blue Pontiac Laurentian station wagon, a huge car like a mobile cave riding on four whitewall tires; the blue of a girl's eyes, eyes like two limpid pools of blue water, eyes I believed I could swim in; and the blue haze that filled the air in a multitude of places. Blue-tinged, tobacco-laden air in rooms and halls was common, accepted along with the walls, windows, and doors. Most rooms floated in a misty haze of blue smoke. The air in restaurants, bars, airplanes, offices, school staff rooms, and cars was blue. Even, and this is the truth, the air in the doctor's office was blue, where ashtrays overflowed with butts, and the doctor's own fingers were often coloured nicotine orange, like carrots.

Now why, you may ask, do I bring up the topics of blue-hazed air and cigarettes? A confession: I smoked. As a callow youth from the age of fifteen, I was taken in by the lying litany of Madison Avenue; by the hero worship of a smoking movie star who always got his girl in the movie, always with a cigarette dangling from his lips; and, most of all, by the pull of the guys I hung with, for fear of being rejected by the boys whose approval and acceptance I desperately needed and craved. They smoked, and so did I. And to its eternal shame, the tobacco industry spent millions to entice countless fifteen-year-olds to become members of the "Smokers' Club." Consequently, lives were destroyed by cancer, emphysema, heart attacks, circulatory problems, all resulting in preventable surgery and death and, often, an earlier-than-planned visit to the local funeral home and cemetery plot. And the tobacco industry knew this but still peddled its poison to impressionable fifteen-year-olds, simply to replace those who had died at age fifty or fifty-five, coughing out their last breaths as they still lit up, sometimes while inhaling pure oxygen from a canister at the same time.

My Dad was a confirmed non-smoker and an almost, but not quite, confirmed teetotaler, hence the lack of liquor bottles and the pristine clarity of the air in our house. Mother, on the other hand, came from a coughing, wheezing tribe of addicted heavy smokers. Consequently, Mother did on occasion puff at a cigarette at parties, especially when she enjoyed a rare drink or two. She was what one would call a very casual one-pack-a-year smoker. I'm sure she never inhaled. I like to think she just liked the movie-star image it gave her. She could be just like Greta Garbo, only with an English accent. As for me, I joined her familial tribe of smokers and was well and truly hooked and addicted to nicotine by my sixteenth birthday.

We smoked mostly "rollies," also known as "roll-your-owns." They were far cheaper but not as sexy as the twenty tailor-made ones I could purchase for thirty-four cents plus a penny match in lieu of change. A tailor-made cigarette was a professional, factory-produced, and much-preferred product. It was perfectly cylindrical from end to end and fitted—oh, so perfectly—inside the soft pack of twenty, which we always then tucked into the left sleeve of the T-shirt we wore as part of our "He's a rebel" uniform. And sexy it was, in the company of a young lady, to remove the pack of twenty cigarettes from the left sleeve of the T-shirt, tap out a cigarette, put the cigarette in the lips, replace the pack carefully into the left sleeve of the T-shirt, and then, with the flourish of a conjurer, flip open the Zippo lighter and put the flame against the waiting end of the cigarette. I even perfected opening the Zippo by applying pressure to the top and the bottom of the lighter and squeezing. The top would fly open, and with a flick of the finger, the lighter flamed, the cigarette glowed, and the girls would be amazed. I was a man indeed!

On the other hand, we manufactured most of our cigarettes by ourselves in Norm's little kitchen factory, using a machine that produced three cigarettes at a time. Our tobacco was bought either in pouches or, when flush with cash, in a can. I learned how to roll a single cigarette by hand by placing a string of tobacco down the centre of a paper and rolling it into a kind of tube. We watched the movies, especially westerns, where the hero would place a strand of tobacco in the paper and then—and this is the hard-to-believe part—roll with one hand, ending up with what appeared to be a perfect cigarette. We tried repeatedly to duplicate this, over and over, usually losing most of the tobacco as it fell to the floor. John Wayne had some explaining to do!

To be totally honest, almost none of the girls I knew smoked. Why I believed they would be impressed by my smoking is beyond me now, but I do suspect that, like most males residing in mid-twentieth-century Canada, the girls' fathers smoked, and girls saw male smoking as largely acceptable male behaviour. And, you must remember, at that time, I had seen a host of male actors smoking in the movies I had attended. That behaviour by a Hollywood hero made a deep impression on the inner workings of the cortex of a teenager, including mine. We were duped by Hollywood in collaboration with the tobacco industry.

I did not at first like smoking. But I heroically persevered, despite my fear of being caught by the old man, and within a month, I was hooked. And, my God, I thought I looked sexy, just like the dashing cowboy as seen on the back cover of *Look* or *Life* magazines. The cigarette dangled lazily from the corner of my lips, the curl of blue smoke rising around half-shut eyes. At least, this is what I believed. And by my seventeenth birthday, I graduated beyond cigarettes to their bigger and far more adult brothers: cigars.

We reserved smoking cigars for special occasions, like playing poker or drinking beer, spirits, or cheap wine in the shack in Norm's backyard. We weren't fussy and consumed a variety of beers and ales—whatever was purchased for us. Drinking was always accompanied by our smoking of cigarettes, but within the hour, and two or three beers later, I graduated to cigars. We favoured the plump, full sized inexpensive kind. Each was lit with a flourish from our Zippo, a lighter every one of our friends seemed to own. And as the drinking continued, so did the cigar smoking. By around eleven o'clock, I was inhaling the smoke, right down into the basement of both of my lungs. How on earth my lungs have carried me into my seventh decade is a good question, considering the torment I put them through in the second and third decades of my life. Those evenings passed in a hazy, smoky, unintelligible slurry of brain farts until, inevitably, I passed out, my brain numbed by alcohol poisoning and the deprivation of oxygen to the brain cells by the deep inhaling of oxygen-free cigar smoke.

But the worst moment was still to come, that awful moment when I opened my eyes in the morning. If there was a moment, I wished for death to mercifully take me, it was then. My head was ten times its normal size, I was parched, my eyes hurt from the light that entered through the shack's one tiny window, and my tongue felt like a herd of elephants had taken a poop on it and then, to add insult to injury, set fire to it.

Lying there, on top of my sleeping bag, I then resolved I really didn't want to die and found faith in the way people under stress or under enemy fire do. I asked God to please, please spare me from the spectre of Death who was looking directly at me, staring at my face. I resolved, "So help me, God. I promise, honest, on my life, to never, ever drink again or smoke cigars again." Then the miracle occurred. He spared me! But, of course, another weekend and another case of twenty-four beers and a fresh pack of cigars later would see that oath fly out of the window. It seems that as soon as the moment passes and we are safe, we shamefully forget what we have promised on oath in the first place, and I was no exception!

When Wayne and I were in Grade 12, graduation loomed, and we began to search for a post-secondary institution that would take us from the rough and tumble of Churchill; from the daily bus ride, occasionally with a girl sitting on my lap and enjoying the bumpy ride as much as I; from the comforts of home, where my mother washed my clothes, made my meals, and made life so easy, to go to a university over 1,200 kilometres from home. It was then we both made the decision to abandon cigarettes for the intellectual look of a pipe, filled with aromatic tobacco imported from far-off Holland. We were to join Jack Kerouac's "Beat Generation" who inhabited Churchill's nonexistent and imaginary coffee houses and snapped fingers to poetry with words that made no sense whatsoever. We were going to be hip—at least as hip as it was possible to be in Churchill. We both purchased pipes—Wayne, a traditional brier, a fine example of a pipe. But mine was a modern work of art. It had a brier bowl attached to an aluminum stem attached to a plastic mouthpiece. The aluminum stem, it was claimed, cooled the smoke as it passed from the bowl to the stem to the tongue. We smoked our pipes and convinced ourselves that we looked so much more mature than mere cigarette smokers. We looked at ourselves in mirrors, checked the right place to position the pipes, as we casually held the bowls and talked to imaginary Beat girls in body-hugging black tops, black tight skirts, and black fishnet stockings. After an exhaustive search for a pipe-smoking role model, the only pipe smoker we could find pictures of was Bing Crosby, and we decided that the "White Christmas" guy did not fit in with our images. He was, after all, ancient. And we were, then, young.

And for a week, I worked on my pipe, and Wayne, on his. But the only other person we knew of our age who smoked a pipe faithfully was a classmate nicknamed Sparky, the three of us swimming in a sea of cigarette smokers.

And we never dared to show up in the cigarette smoke–laden pool hall, take out our pipes, and light up. That would be infinitely stupid. I could hear it, even now, from the louts who held up the walls of the building and commented on everything. "Piss off. What the hell's's that thing? Take off before it's part of your face."

So, like prisoners in isolation, segregated from the general population, we smoked our pipes secretly. And then we gave up! To be honest, my tongue felt just as cooked as it had been when I smoked the far more acceptable cigars and got drunk. That, at least, was fun for the first hour.

So, the pipe was abandoned and was probably discarded with twenty or so years of family history when my folks left Churchill in 1972. And as for me, I managed to abandon the yoke of tobacco in 1968. With that monkey off my back, I could once again smell and taste. Food was once again enjoyable, and not something to hurry through so that I could smoke a cigarette with my cup of coffee and probably annoy the non-smokers who were then far too polite to say anything. And the person most responsible for my becoming tobacco free—the person I must thank and who probably gave me years on my life—is my wife. She had no wish to be a smoker's widow in her fifties. She was clear on this issue. She had grown up in a smoker's household and had no intention of carrying on with another smoker in the house—her house. So, for her, I quit. Just like that. No lotions, no potions, just lots and lots of chewing gum, and lots and lots of encouragement, and lots of young love. And the following year, we married. Her gift to me was a healthy life, liberated from the smiling face of the Scottish lassie whose image appeared on every pack of cigarettes, and perhaps an additional twenty-five years and counting. A life sentence, with no time off for good behaviour. A sentence I have been more than glad to serve.

DDT SUPERSTAR

I have no idea how bugs survived in Churchill, but they did. As sure as the sun rises, there they were. And not just a few that popped out for a week or so, sampled the air, concluded it was decidedly too cold, and then popped back in. No! There they were by the hundreds of millions—well, the tens of thousands—and most of them ready to risk life and wing for a tiny bite of me, or you, or even you over there. There were the usual suspects, including the common housefly that made a nuisance of itself around the dinner table. But then, as if to add insult to injury, there was the unexpected—the slippery, slim silverfish. How he arrived in Churchill I have no idea, but there he was thriving, particularly attracted to the steam-heated baseboard radiators that banged and hissed around the edges of the room. Going outdoors was made miserable by the hordes of flying insects that buzzed in the air, their little wings a blur as they lurked around the doors of our houses or hid in the muskeg or in the weeds that grew along the ditches. How they survived the bitter cold of winter and then, Lazarus-like, every summer rose from the cold, swampy depths of muskeg or the ice-cold waters of ponds or ditches, and then made their way to me in particular, I simply don't know. But they did! My old man, a veteran of the Second World War, engaged himself in a personal campaign to protect his family—this time, not from the Axis powers but from the bugs that swarm and bite.

And it would be a war where no prisoners were taken. A war to destroy the multitude of bugs that buzzed around our back door. A total war where any weapon designed by man to win would be used—and used ruthlessly and lethally.

In those days, we mid-twentieth-century dwellers placed our faith in science and in companies that had laboratories full of scientists who, we were told, used that science to make our lives better. And we believed them. The fact is that most people, and that included my old man, did not realize that these companies often cooked the books, lied, or manipulated the truth, and hired friendly scientists to either support or downplay results, depending upon which result was required. Thus, Madison Avenue con men pushed products that possibly they, and certainly the manufacturers, knew to be harmful. For the doubters, just think about cigarettes—and the horrors that tobacco brings. And like sheep to the slaughter, we bought into the lies. We smoked, relaxing before a flickering black-and-white television that periodically extolled the pleasures and virtues a cigarette could bring, while Grandpa coughed and wheezed in the bathroom. Meanwhile, we used deodorant or hair spray with a propellant that produced holes in the ozone layer. Who knew?

In the meantime, asbestos was pedalled as a product that was nothing less than a gift from the gods. It was everywhere, inescapable, and we scattered it like seeds, with gay abandon. Without any breathing protection, Dad and his crews covered boilers with a fine-powdered cement laced with the stuff. He also covered hot water and steam pipes with tubes of asbestos as insulation, and, as a sixteen-year-old, I blew out truck brake drums with an air hose. Nobody bothered to tell me that brake drums were full of asbestos. And frequently, Dad and I cut out sheets of the stuff to use as a protective fire shield behind exposed heat sources. Nobody said, "Don't do that. It'll kill you for sure." To my old man, asbestos was just another tool in his toolbox. His shop was awash with the stuff. Sheets of it. Bags of it in powdered cement form. Tubes of it to be cut into convenient lengths to insulate pipes. And nobody with even a hint of scientific knowledge said that the stuff was dangerous. And yet—and I'll bet a month's pension—somebody knew the truth and didn't tell.

So, let's return to the topic at hand: how the Churchill locals took on the flying insect population, assisted of course by the bug-killing products manufactured by the chemical industry. To counter the bug population, a periodic spraying around town became a fact of life. This should have been where common sense would be used by the powers that be. The spraying should have been a nocturnal event, when the kiddies, adults, dogs, and cats were safely tucked in their beds, with windows tightly closed to keep out the vapours of the lethal cloud of petroleum-based insecticide. Instead, to the best of my memory at least because nobody seemed to consider the long-term effects of inhaling the particles of insecticide, spraying took place at—well—basically anytime. And to make the situation even more interesting, the local radio station announced where and when the spraying would take place on that day, presumably so that responsible people would keep pets and kiddies indoors and close the windows to avoid the noxious ethers. But unfortunately, this public service announcement was as a flame to moths; kids ages five to fifteen would gather at the announced starting point to await the arrival of the spraying truck. When the spraying commenced, an evil-smelling, diesel-enhanced giant white cloud would appear, and the kids in turn would disappear into that white cloud. The kids then, like a school yard gang, followed the white cloud, shrieking and yelling and, in the process, deeply inhaling the vapour as they ducked into it and were again swallowed by the cloud. And nobody stopped them. I wonder, many years later, how these kids fared, and I think of the possible health problems they may have encountered. Can you say "emphysema" or "cancer"?

Dad welcomed the arrival of the spraying truck, as it did, temporarily at least, allow him to go outside to a bug-free yard and work on his car. Between sprays, though, he was still at war with insects. And like most people, he was reassured by the chemical industry and by Madison Avenue that life would be perfect if he "lived better chemically." This was the war cry of the chemical industry. Advertising implored us to live better chemically. Environmentalists were demonized as wild-eyed crackpots, and Dad, not to put too fine a point on it, was not an environmentalist. He put his faith in science, and his favourite weapon of choice to kill bugs was DDT—because it worked!

Dad had somehow managed to scrounge and stockpile cans of DDT, all labelled "Property of the US Army." Where he got these cans, I have absolutely no idea. And I never asked. I really didn't want to know. And as he has long since passed on, as has his source, I will never know. The cans were khaki, the same colour as uniforms, jeeps, and trucks. They were identical in size and shape to aerosol cans found in stores, cans dispensing shaving cream, hair spray, or furniture polish. But his US Army cans were plain, with the letters DDT and a part number printed on the side. There was no need to make the product look pretty. No colours, no slogans like "Mountain Air Fresh" or "Lemon Scented," and no pictures of a breeze blowing flimsy white curtains through a window that looked out upon a flower-festooned pasture. Instead, out from the dispenser came a cloud of evil-smelling white vapour that did, indeed, kill on contact. It was great stuff. We rarely had a fly, mosquito, spider, or silverfish once the old man discovered the wonderful world of DDT. He even took cans of the stuff to our cottage, which could be bug paradise, especially at night when the lights of our cottage attracted a veritable zoo of weird-looking things with wings. They hung around the outside of the window and longingly looked in. And they were the lucky ones. Any that managed to get into our modest lakeside cottage met the same DDT fate—instant chemically induced death.

When Mum and Dad passed on, Val and I disposed of the remaining stock of Dad's armoury. But, and here the story gets interesting, what impressed me was the potency of the DDT residue. We had large windows looking out onto the lake, windows scrounged by Dad from a shop that had been renovated in Swan River, a nearby town. The inside wooden windowsill had never been painted and, in the past, had been liberally sprayed with Dad's DDT as a part of his war on bugs. As a testament to science, the windowsill still managed to kill flies. The flies would alight on the sill, wander around, and then begin to walk in wobbly circles, like little drunks, and then roll over with their little legs in the air.

And yes, these bugs are still stubbornly with us, despite the best efforts of the chemical companies and Dad's ferocious assault with his cache of DDT. They are still with us. Adapting. Learning to survive and fight back. Dad may have won his little battles, but we are collectively losing the war. And it is a war we are losing on many fronts, from crop failures to deforestation, from droughts to massive floods, largely caused by global warming, accelerated by our addiction to fossil fuels. Dad would now be horrified to see how the world has changed.

Dad would be horrified to see how the world has changed because he was hoodwinked, just as I was hoodwinked by the tobacco manufacturers.

We will never defeat Mother Nature. Nor should we. She is so much smarter than we. I have been told that the ice-free season has grown by two weeks at each end when compared to the 1950s and the world I knew. If true, this is catastrophic to the planet.

And one more salient thing to think about: this gives the insects four more weeks to do whatever it is that insects like to do. We really did lose that war, didn't we?

LIFE IN A NORTHERN TOWN

I was not born northern. Far from it. I have, in truth, lived much of my life on the "outside"—a term used in the North to describe the South. Nevertheless, I have long considered myself—buried deep in my soul—a northerner by default. Now you may ask, how can this be? Well, the answer is simply put. Those teenaged years I spent in that gritty subarctic community were the genesis of me, the vital years that saw a callow, mirror-obsessed youth become the responsible adult I am today. Those years were the very years when the "wiring" of the brain that we all apparently go through was just about completed. And I say "just about" because neither I nor my incredibly patient wife are sure it was finished. Those then were the years when the "I" became the more inclusive "we." Those were the years when my personality, for good or ill, evolved.

Winter, not surprisingly, is the season that most dominates northern life and leaves an indelible stamp on the development and maturing of a young mind. I learned early that there exist two faces to winter. On one side, a haunting beauty. On the other, danger—even death.

There were three teenagers who thought they were immortal, who made what—in retrospect—was a silly decision to cross, by foot, the heaved tidal ice of the Churchill River estuary on a sharp, clear, sunny, cold, ice blue–skied Sunday morning in February, just to get to the other side. My friends and I were those teenagers. And I may note here, we told nobody where we were off to. I don't really think we knew initially where we were off to. We just impulsively set off and, thankfully, came back in one piece. Luck was with us then. The weather held when it may have changed. We made it home, and my parents would have been none the wiser had it not been for a call from Wayne's parents. wondering if my parents knew of an unannounced hike across a frozen river to the fort that day. As Desi would say to Lucy on the *I Love Lucy* show, "You have some 'splainin' to do."

As a youngster, I recall our small frame house shuddering with the power of the wind gusting unabated off the ice of the bay. I also recall staring at the blowing snow being lifted and blown around, creating a surface blizzard, even though no new snow had fallen. The wind-driven swirl consisted entirely of existing snow rising and stretching and readjusting itself, creating new snowbanks where none had previously existed, piling up and over Dad's beloved '57 Ford Ranchero parked in the yard and, as if by magic, making old snowbanks disappear.

Our dog, a creature of careless interbreeding by opportunistic forebears, was, like all dogs, a creature of habit. When nature called, he would pace by the door, and when the door was opened, he would escape temporarily into the wind-driven, snow-driven world. To satisfy his dog ritual, he would sniff and then circle the same spot, and then, with a great show of satisfaction, proceed to pee. But being a dog, he did not comprehend the power of the wind's ability to erase his personal snowbank. Perplexed, he wandered around, nose held close to the surface of the snow and, finally, in complete surrender, picked a new place. I'm sure, deep within the cortex of his doggy brain, because he was not a particularly intelligent dog to begin with, he did not understand, and there was both confusion and resentment because he was somehow being tricked into finding a new spot to pee. Dogs are such simple, one-faceted creatures. That's why they love us unconditionally.

Even today, I still vividly remember awakening on frigid January mornings and seeing, through half-shut eyes, my breath as I exhaled and upon pulling at my sheets and bedding, finding them frozen to the walls as the wind hammered and shook the house. This, along with the frost that formed perilously around the electrical outlets, and the gradual thickening in the layer of ice on the surface of drafty windows, was the true herald that winter had an increasingly firm grip on my world.

I recall walking to catch the school bus on bitterly cold mornings, wearing my dark blue surplus USAF parka that I had purchased by mail from the Army and Navy Surplus store in Winnipeg, wearing it with the hood—by absolute necessity—covering my ears, head, and most of my face so that only my eyes could be seen through the hood's man-made fur trim. My breath, held captive in the space between my mouth and the rim of the hood, would condense and freeze in successive layers on the fur, forming a white rim. My frozen eyelashes would also become increasingly coated with ice, forcing me to periodically take off a mitt and pick the ice from my lashes.

The townsite itself was primitive. Drainage ditches, carrying water-borne diseases such as hepatitis, lined the sides of gravel roads that blew with clouds of dust as vehicles passed on hot, dry summer days. With spring, the snow in the ditches yielded to the ever-strengthening sun. And with the melt, I recall seeing emerge boxes; rusting pieces of iron, once part of something useful; tired, worn tires; bits of paper and cardboard; and, even more alarming, the occasional dog—dead as a dodo and frozen until the sun did its work. Little wonder hepatitis occasionally made its way around town with the spring. Yellow eyes and skin were practically accepted as normal.

"Bill won't be here for a while, sir," we'd say to the teacher. "He's got hepatitis."

And Bill would be home, sometimes, for weeks.

And in the summer, the air was perfumed by the odour of what polite society called "night soil." Why human waste was called "night soil" but the droppings of your dog, I believe quite appropriately, were called "dog poop" is beyond me. But regardless of whatever you chose to call it—and for the more genteel among us, I'll call it night soil—it was still disgusting, collected over the period of a day or two in a bucket equipped with a steel handle and a round wooden grip, and removed from the "bathroom" of the house. It was then carried very carefully to the yard, where awaited a wooden crib, covering a hole of some kind into which the night soil was delicately poured. "Don't splash it," you'd mutter to yourself.

It is hard, using the lens of time, to conclude which was the best or worst season of the year to dispose of the night soil. All I know is that whatever the season, it often fell to me to empty the bucket. Winter saw the contents of the crib frozen and less perfumed, but the ice around the crib made the task slippery and walking an adventure. Summer saw huge swarms of flies and an odour that could quite literally knock your socks off. Of the two, I do believe

I favoured winter, although I did once slip and fall while carrying the bucket. Mother simply disposed of the clothing I was wearing and promptly stuck my backside in a tub of hot water.

The fact that winter occupied at least six months of the calendar meant that the other three seasons had to share the remaining six. Thus, during this brief respite from winter, nature took care of business. The fox pursues the vixen, the goose, the gander. Mr. Lemming searches out his missus, and plants bud, grow, flower, and seed. And all hope that enough was done to perpetuate the species—at least, that is, until the next year.

And we were busy too! Summer drove some to escape to the "outside" and reassure themselves that a real world awaited beyond the bubble of Churchill. And summer was when things were started, and hopefully finished, in the long, sunlit days of May, June, July, and August. These long days gave more daylight hours to build new structures, demolish old ones, repair roads, and tar roofs. Goods flooded in by rail and sea. Railed-in grain left for Europe in huge freighters. Oil and fuel were tankered in. Goods were transhipped further north to meet the winter needs of remote communities. And, as I found to my surprise and dismay, there were graves to be dug—to accommodate those who were to die but were unaware of it.

And every season saw the military—primarily Canadian and American but sometimes British or German—train, evaluate equipment, cold-weather test aircraft, and prepare for a war with the Soviets that nobody wanted but, on occasion, came perilously close to engaging in and have so far, thankfully, avoided.

Churchill was a place where advanced research into the aurora borealis was conducted. Hundreds of rockets were hurled into space for just that purpose. And while this was happening, giant helium-filled balloons were launched, balloons that rose and grew in size as they expanded, eventually looking like a bright new star in the evening sky. In the meantime, to prepare for World War III, the USAF constructed a runway capable of landing a B-52 bomber, and a hangar to house one. And a giant military base was constructed to house thousands of military personnel and their families—a modern complex with all the amenities of a small town.

Today, it is all gone, a sacrificial token offered to the bulldozer gods, except for recognizable remnants. I am reminded of Shelley's poem "Ozymandias," in which a traveller describes a king of an ancient land whose shattered statue lies half buried in sand. On the pedestal of the statue are inscribed the words:

"My name is Ozymandias, King of Kings.

Look on my Works, ye Mighty, and despair!"

Shelley goes on, noting:

Nothing beside remains. Round the decay

Of that colossal Wreck, boundless and bare

The lone and level sands stretch far away.

Today, snow swirls and whirls around empty spaces where once, as a boy, I played and experienced life. Now all is gone, just a vacant space where boys and girls courted each other, went to school and to the movies, where people made love, had kids, and lived. And some even died to occupy one of those waiting graves.

So, there it is. Despite the many years I have lived and worked on the "outside," I am still a northerner—as I said—by default. It shaped me. And sometimes, even now, as I stand and watch the autumn leaves fall while a watery sun attempts to light the room, I am transported back through the years and decades to a time that was my time, a time that echoes and reverberates in my memory, a time that will never be repeated. As Shelley said, "Nothing beside remains." There is no need to say more.

YESTERDAY WHEN I WAS YOUNG

Today, as I wandered one of the larger shopping malls in town, ostensibly to get a little exercise, something I am likely to do only on rare occasions, I observed a lady walking toward me. Because I was in a busy location, this was not, of course, out of the ordinary. To be honest, ladies seemed to outnumber men in the mall, and there were probably dozens of them heading in my direction. What set this lady apart from the others, some of whom I would be wary of meeting alone in a dark alley, was that this lady was laughing, talking loudly, and gesturing in the company of nobody. She was all alone. In my youth, such a person would be removed, albeit gently, by gentlemen in white coats driving a white van and waving huge butterfly nets. In my youth, these gentlemen would have probably concluded that she was not in her right mind. Upon passing the lady, curious about this behaviour on her part, I could not resist a shy sideways glance and saw a thing, a device of some sort, attached to her ear. What was it? Upon inquiry, my sons, who are part of this new, magical electronics age of iPhones, informed me that she was probably using a communication device, perhaps a telephone. I have no doubt that my boys were correct. I confess, I am a Luddite in the mysterious world of cybertechnology. My sons, born of the cyber era, are not. And this lady, apparently, wasn't either, as she was having a lively conversation with somebody, perhaps as far away as Hong Kong. All that I do know is just how much my world has evolved and changed since I was in short pants, changes sometimes for the better and sometimes, regretfully, not.

Let me illustrate this for you. In my youthful days, sixty-odd years ago, we never, ever—just as the world turns daily without fail on its axis—called our friends' parents by their first names, either in person or over the telephone.

This would never, ever enter our minds. Oh, we certainly knew their first names. But it was always "Mr. This" or "Mrs. That." And let me make this clear. The gang of guys I hung out with had parents who indeed had names we once called "Christian names"—which have since, perhaps for the better, morphed into the more politically correct "given names"—and these names were never, ever uttered by us in public. We did this out of respect. That was the way of the times. It was always, "Good morning, Mrs. L, and may I say how pretty you look today." Actually, I never said that part. That was a lie. But she was an attractive woman in a motherly and mature sort of way.

The values of the mid-twentieth-century world were so different and, may I suggest, less democratic than today. Want an example? I currently volunteer two days a week at a museum, an act of apparent altruism but in reality, to keep me in the loop with what day of the week it is. Otherwise, my week would consist of seven Saturdays in a row. But I digress. At this museum, I encounter harried mothers or exasperated grannies desperately trying to control children who are obviously a) out of control and b) in the driver's seat. It is there I will hear mothers or grannies trying to reason with an unreasonable four-year-old. And I say "unreasonable" not in a bad way but because they are four-year-olds, and four-year-olds are naturally unreasonable. Thus, I hear a mother pleading, "Get out of there, Simon. I said *GET OUT!*" And Simon must be pulled, losing his boots in the struggle, out of wherever he was. And what of little Brittany? Cute as a button and already world-wise, Brittany is perhaps three and a half and clutches a stuffed pink bunny. In Brittany's eyes, you can see that same Churchillian defiance we saw in Winston's eyes in 1941 as he stood on the beach and stared across the English Channel at Hitler. Brittany is with her Nana, who enquires of Brittany, "What shall we do next, Brittany? You want to go where? Sorry, Mummy said no fast food. Stop screaming, Brittany! Don't you dare throw that, Brittany! Don't you dare! LISTEN TO ME!"

The stuffed pink bunny takes wings and flies, and Brittany throws herself, like a sack of potatoes, onto the floor, leaving nana to hoist the sobbing child onto her rubbery legs and feet and retrieve the stuffed bunny before setting off for a hamburger and chips.

It appears to me that adults believe four-year-olds can function as if in an adult-to-adult relationship and can make rational, adult decisions. Well, sorry to say, they can't. In the mid-'50s, as kids, we were told what to do and where to go, like it or lump it. Choices were rarely handed out, and those that were—such as, "What would you like for Christmas?"—we treasured. What we wanted and what we actually got were not always the same thing.

We grew up in a post–World War II atmosphere of austerity, and my friends and I lived with parents who had been separated for three, four, or even five years. Dads were away because of wartime duty, and mums worked for good wages, employed in wartime factories riveting together planes, tanks, and ships. Upon returning from duty, these dads—strangers to the kids and sometimes to the wives they had left behind, with minds sometimes haunted by what they had seen in Italy or France—doggedly re-created a 1930s household, two decades late, in the 1950s, homes made up of the traditional pre-war wife and children who were all too often subjected to the traditional pre-war life of paternalistic domination. Life for these kids and for the wives was not so wonderful. In fact, it could be awful, even brutal. The wartime world of financial and personal independence of just mother and kids ended with a thud! Fairly strict social values were reimposed. The wife, often reluctantly, was once again pushed into her role, once again held hostage in the house, tied to the kitchen sink and enslaved by the stove.

And what of the kids? They resided in a paternalistic kingdom until each came of age, which usually meant when he or she left the house or could vote, whichever came first. Each child occupied a place on the lowest rung of the family ladder of life. The addition of a succession of postwar siblings meant that the rung became quite crowded. Graduation from high school may have allowed some to tentatively step up onto a second rung, but, in the dictates of the time, this was not a guaranteed given. And you remained anchored to your rung on the family's ladder of life until it was decided by some unwritten law, controlled usually by the father, with no wordy constitution to confuse the issue, that you could move up. You could then commence to climb the ladder, being careful not to step on others, especially on doddery grandparents who were becoming increasingly dependent upon their children and were on their way down. And, if truth be told, I was more than content with this arrangement, an arrangement that was universal in the western world, whether living in subarctic Churchill, like me, or in gay Paris, like Brigitte Bardot. Most kids everywhere knew their places, whether at home, in the classroom, in our local pool hall (where miscreant behaviour was common, even expected), or in church (where it definitely was not). Misbehaviour in church meant not only parental wrath but also the wrath of the deity, a scary guy in the sky who casts thunderbolts at bad people. Or even worse, the threat of the devil, Old Nick himself, grabbing you and dragging you off to perpetual fire and brimstone to roast you with his giant toasting fork stuck in your arse. Oh, there were always kids who thought they knew better, but usually a good swipe or glare, or both, solved the problem. Most mid-'50s kids lived in a regulated world where parental law superseded the laws of the land. Not that we kids didn't kick over the traces on occasion and, in the spirit of Marlon Brando or James Dean, rebel by looking at magazines our parents disapproved of or smoking in the pool hall, which our parents disapproved of. But that was about as far as things would go. That is, until I met Norm and Wayne.

We first met in September in the town square, waiting for the school bus—at the bus stop near the Hudson's Bay store next to the flagpole with the weather-worn Red Ensign fluttering above, and in front of the two cannons which in all likelihood would, if fired, be more dangerous to the gunners than to the enemy. We were on our way to school on the first day of a brand-new school year. We clicked immediately, and within a week, it was as if we had been lifelong chums. We formed for ourselves a society of like-minded gentlemen. We shared common interests and shared golden nuggets of incredible information about the strange, terrifying, exciting new world that was just waiting to be discovered.

Now, at this juncture in my ramble through time, I must emphasize that most of these nuggets were baseless, simply not true, yet we shared them breathlessly, treated them like holy relics, which, by the way, were also baseless. There are probably enough slivers of wood from the Cross of Calvary floating around in medieval cathedrals capable of building an entire medieval village.

Yes, when I first met Norm and Wayne, I knew I was "in." And that, as the saying goes, was that! There was that curt, manly understanding between three boys, and our interests were amazingly similar. It was uncanny how alike we were. Our conversations often revolved around girls, a subject that filled many an hour. Music kicked in occasionally. We agreed we hated country, loved doo-wop, and listened to Winnipeg's CKY Radio 58 when reception permitted, the home of "Manitoba's Friendly Giant." We believed that Fabian was a pretty boy who couldn't sing a note, and we couldn't understand the female infatuation with him, but our estimation of him rose slightly when he played opposite to John Wayne in the movie *North to Alaska*. I loved Brenda Lee. I loved "I'm Sorry." I imagined she was singing an apology to me. And so it went, artful discussion on topics that really mattered. And all the time, we lived under the dark, obscene shadow of the bomb. Not any old bomb but *the* bomb. We knew what it could do from cinema newsreels. We had been exposed to the famously inept "duck and cover" propaganda, put forth by lying politicians well-schooled in Orwellian logic, a fairy tale suggesting that if you fell to your knees under a desk and put your hands over your head, you could protect yourself from a thermonuclear blast. We knew, of course, by our fourteenth birthdays that it was utter nonsense. We also knew that the world balanced insanely on a knife's edge, our survival depended upon just how crazy the political boss in Moscow or Washington was. This was constantly driven home to us by the sound of military muscle, the sound of American aircraft as they took off, landed, and took off again from Churchill's brand new, US-funded runway that many of the guys I knew laboured on for $2.75 an hour instead of completing high school.

We were terrified by the insane nuclear circus we were forced to participate in. Then in 1959, we saw the movie *On the Beach*. And in case you wondered, no, this is not a "beach blanket bingo" movie featuring Annette Funicello romping in the sand with her cute smile and bikini. This movie described a post-apocalyptic world that scared the wits out of us. This was a world where all of us in the northern hemisphere would be dead because of a nuclear war, while Gregory Peck, the crew of his submarine, and the folks in far-off Australia were patiently waiting to die from radiation sickness. "What the hell?" we'd say. Bravado in words of futile defiance.

Yes, it was a topsy-turvy world we inhabited—a world where the practice of racial inequality, of racial superiority, was drilled into the minds of children and believed by parents, spurred on by scheming politicians who feasted upon ignorance, despite having just fought fascism in a war to free the world from lies, hatred, and tyranny. Ours was a world where, in an odd pyrrhic way, we were also prepared to exterminate ourselves in a quest to "save democracy."

And as for us boys, we lived in a simpler world. A world where we called our male teachers "Sir" and all female teachers, regardless of marital status, "Miss." And when, on a lucky streak, we were on a date, we boys nodded politely as a girl's father rightfully told us in no uncertain terms to "Have Sheila home by ten. No later. You understand, young man?" This was always followed by a respectful, "Yes, sir." But being fifteen or sixteen and beginning to demonstrate a streak of free will and independence, we made sure Sheila got home by 10:15 p.m. This was our world, a world where you knew your place on the family ladder, rebelled when you could, and, unlike today, never talked aloud to an invisible person unless you really were crazy and the men in white coats with the white van came searching for you with large butterfly nets.

I have long learned that the passage of time has a way of giving a rosy tint to those years that were sometimes terrifying, a time when the Cold War was in full swing, when the world tottered insanely on the edge of oblivion. As a youngster, I absorbed this as I listened to the news on the CBC. And although the news, as did life itself, travelled at a slower pace than today, those times were no less frightening nor less dangerous. It was via radio I learned of the atmospheric testing of thermonuclear bombs by both the Soviets and the Americans and that this testing produced an atmospheric cloud of drifting radioactive strontium-90, a cloud that knew no borders and was indiscriminate. Strontium-90 found its way, via rain and snow, into the soil, worked its way into the grass, was eaten by the cows who produced milk, and—voila—radioactive bottles of milk appeared on the shelves of supermarkets, milk that was consumed by children. And strontium-90 behaved like calcium, burying itself into the bones and teeth of growing children, like Jimmy or Mary, both of whom would later die from an assortment of bomb-induced cancers. Goodbye, Jimmy. Sorry, Mary, you could have been so beautiful. Largely because of this, the atmospheric testing of bombs was banned, but subterranean testing has continued. Out of sight, out of mind, I must presume.

The years since that time, the time of my youth, have slipped by and, somehow, we have survived, more by luck than by skill. And if we are lucky and common sense prevails, my three beautiful granddaughters, a half century from now, as I have done, will also look back and, like me, wonder how their generation managed to muddle through. God willing, I hope they do. After all, the alternative is unthinkable.

SHADOW DANCING, 1962-1970

The beginning of the end of my daily routine, my day-to-day life in that end-of-the-line northern town, began on that day in mid-July when I picked up my final Grade 12 examination marks from the family's post office box—the very same box that connected us to the outside world of blue aerograms from relatives in the UK, connected Dad to his mail-in record club, connected Mother to her precious lifeline in the form of a steady seasonal procession of Eaton's catalogues, and connected me to the happy optician in Winnipeg who regularly replaced my lost or broken eyeglasses.

I had already determined that furthering my education elsewhere was, in my mind, a safe choice, as I could put off for at least a year, and perhaps even by two or three, the necessity of choosing a vocation. School in the south would also take me from home, hundreds of kilometres away, to a new place with new people and, hopefully, new friends. I was, in a sense, kicking the what-to-do-with-my-life can down the path, optimistically hoping that options would, by some miracle or two, fall into place. I was not what one would call a "life planner" but a "life chancer." And, as a comforting thought, I would not leave home entirely, as with the passing of each academic year, I would still trek home each summer for four months of well-paid employment and home-cooked meals and properly washed laundry and would also be home for a couple of weeks over the holidays at Christmas. And, yes, at first, I still regarded the old town as home. But slowly—tick, tick, tick— those ties were to be weakened by forces over which I had little control. And I was to establish new roots elsewhere that would initially be hesitant and frail but later take a firm hold in soil of my choosing.

The three years to complete my BA flew by, and by graduation, I still had no idea what I wanted to do for either temporary or permanent employment. After all, what does a BA really prepare a person for? Then came serendipity. Or was it divine intervention? It matters not, because the answer to this conundrum came as a response to a serious teacher shortage in Manitoba. It appeared that virtually anybody with a degree—and who was not regarded as a child molester—could go into a classroom and teach unsuspecting children. The shortage was so acute that the province was paying the university tuition fees for qualified individuals and covered the first year of the two-year Bachelor of Education program. Never having considered being a teacher and unsure I really wanted to be a teacher, I nevertheless applied and was, to my surprise, immediately accepted. I do not recall ever having an interview. It was that easy. Just a jaunty, "Sign on the line, John," and I was in. And one academic year later, there I was, a newly minted professional teacher granted a provisional licence, legally allowed to stand before Grade 12 students, many of whom were barely younger than me, and attempted to do what my teachers had tried to do for me just a few years prior. Now the proverbial shoe was on the other foot.

The 1960s were a time of political upheaval, social change, and chaos both in Canada and in the neighbouring republic to the south, which was twisting like a pretzel on a string in the breeze from the fight over civil rights, and actively showing revulsion over the war in Vietnam that we saw on the television news every night.

In addition, we at home in Canada experienced a whirlwind called "Trudeaumania," and young people, excited by politics, were sucked into the vortex. At the same time, there was a whiff of homegrown revolution blowing in the winds. *The Front de libération du Québec* (FLQ), Quebec separatists, were in the business of annoying the federal government, blowing up mailboxes, kidnapping a British diplomat, and finally graduating to murdering a Quebec politician. In the United States, young Americans, fed up with the killing fields of Vietnam and refusing to be drafted into the army, voted with their feet, and hurried north on unfamiliar roads, looking for sanctuary. Canada became the new home and haven for them. I taught with one, an exiled American, a colleague in my school with a strange-sounding accent who just wanted peace and to be left alone to live his life.

Then by chance, I met a twenty-year-old student nurse. Princess Serendipity had on a whim, waved her wand. I was immediately drawn to her dark, penetrating eyes and to her very different Ukrainian roots. I had never known a girl quite like her. And, not to overstate the obvious, like many Ukrainian girls, she was attractive—an attraction, I might add, that was reciprocated. Not to overuse the cliché, but we were a case of opposites attract.

The late '60s was the age of Aquarius, the pill, Woodstock, flower power, and San Francisco and free love—a time when authority was rejected in a haze of smoke that was probably not tobacco. It was also the time when women, yearning for sexual equality, burned their bras, marched, and celebrated a newfound freedom with the miniskirt, apparel that shrank shorter by the month, a garment that allowed the sun to shine on parts where the sun had never publicly shone before.

We men, not to be outdone, chose to grow our hair longer, cultivate extravagant sideburns and moustaches, wear collarless Nehru jackets introduced from Britain by The Beatles, wear platform shoes with two-inch-thick soles, and wear trousers with bell bottoms that mushroomed in size almost weekly. I purchased "far out" trousers with vertical white and red stripes, very fashionable for the times. In retrospect, I think they were manufactured from excess window-awning material.

This generation was to be influenced by all things British: accents, haircuts, the Mini motorcar, "I Want to Hold Your Hand" and The Beatles," Twiggy, "Wild Thing" and The Troggs, Carnaby Street fashion, "The House of the Rising Sun" and The Animals, Michael Caine, London, and Liverpool—the latter, a gritty port city attached by nautical routes to all things American, a city that most young Americans had probably never heard of a couple of years earlier but became the working-class heartbeat of some of the greatest music of the twentieth century.

Now let's get back to that pretty nurse I met in 1968. We dated, fell in love, and just over a year later, married in the summer of '69, a very good year, except neither of us had any money. But we both had brand-new jobs that gave us the ability to purchase a very small brand-new Japanese car, which promptly began to rust away. Those jobs also enabled us to rent a small, brand new, one-bedroom flat, furnished in the affordable minimalistic style—without a TV. After all, when you were a brand new, newlywed couple, the lack of a TV turned out to be irrelevant. Initially, filling those empty hours was easy, with afternoon and evening delights, focused on each other. All was sunshine and roses, youthful play reluctantly interspersed with required work so that we could pay the rent and eat. Paying the rent and buying food and paying for the instalments on the car consumed all our wages.

Then in the autumn of '69, as if the fates had decided that our happiness was too much for them to tolerate, we were burgled, while at work earning enough so that we could pay the rent and eat. The little we owned was stolen, replaced by the sick feeling in the stomach, replaced by the revulsion that someone had gone through our few possessions. A broken door lock, scattered drawers pulled from furniture in haste, and strewn clothing was the evidence. Val, who rarely left her engagement ring anywhere but on her ring finger, had been told days before not to wear her ring on duty because, as the evening supervisor advised, "Rings are full of germs and microbes and not conducive to the health of patients." So, she took it off and left it at home when she left for work. It was stolen by some wretch from the top drawer of the new chest of drawers in the bedroom where Val had innocently put it, along with a container filled with old coins Val's dad had given her and cash we had collected from our friends and family to purchase, of all things, Tupperware, at a friend's upcoming Tupperware party—a party where ladies drank coffee and tea, ate dainties, and passed around plastic containers. Thus, Val not only lost an uninsured ring but also had to replace the money she'd collected and ended up buying her family's and our friends' Tupperware. We were naive, broke, and without household insurance coverage. After all, who would want to steal the next to nothing we owned? That had not even been on our radar. Val's solitaire engagement ring, that had been engraved with our names, was replaced four years later; it was beautiful but never the same. And the Tupperware? I believe it has long since gone into an eternal home called "Tupperware heaven," to frolic forever, watched over by a plastic deity shaped like an airtight box, to frolic with all the other lidless Tupperware pieces. Our tiny, brand new, perfect, sparsely furnished one-bedroom apartment was no longer perfect, the intimacy gone and replaced by the spectre of someone rifling through our personal things, all spoiled by the ruffian who broke in and took what little we had of value. Val found it difficult to sleep there alone during the day when I was away teaching after she had completed a night shift at the hospital. Can't say I could blame her; I would feel the same. She took to sometimes going to her parents' home to sleep. This sense of violation was, of course, long before the advent of modern security systems. The only answer to this was to move somewhere else as soon as the lease expired in the following year. And we did just that, with the help of my old man, my mother, their enormous Pontiac Laurentian station wagon, Val's parents and her dad's cavernous Chevrolet Impala, and anybody else willing to carry what little we owned: china cups and plates and cutlery in boxes, an assortment of pots and pans, bedding and comforters, a bed frame and mattress and box spring, a large dresser and mirror, a chest of drawers, a bookcase, a yellow French Provincial couch and armchair with wooden grips on the end of the padded arms that looked to me like perfect little coffins, a coffee table, two side tables, a telephone table, dining table and four Scandinavian-styled chairs, a variety of lamps and table linens that we had received as wedding gifts, our clothing, and toiletries. That was it! Everything we owned.

Our next apartment was located across the river in Fort Rouge, a higher end and, we certainly hoped, less petty-criminal-inhabited part of the city. This apartment was a wee bit larger but still with one bedroom—and a little more expensive. However, a small increase in our salaries helped pay the difference. Our apartment was what agents loved to call a "character apartment." This meant that it was older, the windows leaked cold air in winter, and without air conditioning, the place was predictably hot in the July and August dog days of summer. And we loved it!

At the same time, my parents and Churchill were on my mind. I had seen them both that summer, and I kept in touch via the telephone. At that time, my dad was obviously worried about the future. His tone of voice told the story. As for Mother, she was stoic, resigned to the fact that a move was in the cards, looming like a grey cloud over the horizon. The only question was, to where? Things were not going well in Churchill. The optimism of the '50s and '60s yielded to the pessimism of the '70s. The armed forces had made the fatal decision to move out. The American Air Force and Army and the Canadian Air Force, Army, and Navy had all concluded that Churchill was past its "best by" date, and the testing, training, and spying could all be conducted elsewhere, as could the research. The US Air Force had by then developed air refuellers that no longer needed to use Churchill as a base and had moved these resources back to the States. All that was left behind was a shell of something that had once supported a large military complex. For the moment, the government of Canada decided that the Department of Public Works, where my father was employed, should continue with the maintenance of the buildings, but with its purpose to exist gone, it was only time before the base would be abandoned. And Dad knew this.

Slowly, things began to wind down. The Department of Northern Affairs transformed some of the barrack blocks into dormitories to house Inuit students from the Northwest Territories, but this program was understandably unpopular with parents who lived in communities hundreds of miles from Churchill. It folded after a short run. Dad, sensing the end, and still several years to pension, reluctantly began a search for new horizons. Mother was understandably unhappy at the thought of leaving what had become her home and her friends.

Meanwhile in Winnipeg, the autumn days grew shorter, and Christmas loomed. Val and I were comfortable in our new, but old, flat. Bing was still crooning "White Christmas," and we both happily believed we had everything, except money. And we were not alone. Many of our friends were in the same financial sea as we. To save money, we gathered on weekends, attended movie theatres downtown, watched television, drank cheap red wine or beer, and ate bowls of cheesy bits or chips. The centre of attention in our apartment was a large, heavy, quite erotic black pot. This pot was the creation of Val's skilled cousin, Ken, a local artist and two other talented local artists. We stored it for him, and people would get onto their hands and knees and slowly turn it just to see what the people on the pot were up to. And I use the word "up" quite deliberately and literally. We both manoeuvred this pot into the bedroom and hid it under a sheet whenever Val's parents visited. Val was never sure how her mother, especially, would react to the behaviours on display on the pot.

Some of our friends had summered on a European bus tour, and we were sorely tempted. But being sensible, we both sensibly chose to spend as much time, and as little money, as we could staying with my mother and sister at the new, partially completed family cottage Dad and I were working on in the Duck Mountains. However, we did make the extravagant decision to purchase not a simple black-and-white television but an Admiral console colour TV. This TV, our single most expensive furniture expenditure, had a special "sports switch" that, when clicked on, made the picture a most definite shade of green. It did, of course, make the football field look excellent but gave the ice surface of hockey rinks a peculiar hue. And the TV, full of glowing tubes, was incredibly heavy. It needed two healthy men just to lift and move it. And as our flat was on the third floor of the apartment block, theft would be very difficult indeed.

Fall turned into the early winter of 1970, and as Christmas approached, Val and I did our shopping, looking for gifts, but still with one eye on the bankbook balance. Yes, banks then gave you books. There were no ATMs, and banking hours were more than inconvenient. We were both working, the normal ten-months-long, five-days-a-week teaching routine; Val, the shift work full-time registered nurses had to accept, and the juggle of days, evenings and nights, weekdays, holidays, weekends, and whatever else the hospital chose to throw at her. We, as newlyweds, found the demands of her work schedule on our personal lives difficult and frustrating.

That second Christmas Eve saw the two of us decorate and then admire our apartment-sized Christmas tree. Rather than purchase a decorative Christmas tree topper, we decided to create our very own tree topper. This we made from the metal stand of a glass tea pot using tin foil to mould a Christmas star. I still treasure photographs of two very young, and dare I say attractive, people sitting by that tree. Val had elected to work Christmas Day and take off New Year's Day, as she was entitled to one or the other, but not both.

As Val was working Christmas Day, and we would both be up very early so that she could dress in her nursing uniform and I could drive her to the hospital for her shift at 7:00 a.m., we elected to open a few of our gifts around eleven in the evening on Christmas Eve. Sitting on the floor beside our glowing evergreen tree, I recall Val looking at me for a long time. Her dark eyes were hard to avoid. Then she asked the question to which I am certain she knew the answer.

"What would be the most perfect Christmas gift for you?" Her eyes flashed. She knew the answer, but I hesitated.

"Home," I finally said. "I'd love to go home." I had not been home for three and a half years. I missed home. I missed my parents. I even missed my little sister whom I hardly knew. She was a complete surprise to everybody— even to my parents. She was truly a gift, and I needed to know her.

So, we decided to try to go to Churchill for the remainder of the Christmas season. And everything that needed to be done to accomplish this trip home to Churchill was done, surprisingly quickly. By December 27, we had returned many of the gifts we'd bought for each other and got a refund. We raided our bank account for extra cash and purchased two roundtrip airline tickets—Winnipeg to Churchill, via Thompson—and by evening, we were at the airport waiting to catch our flight.

I called home and told my parents. Mum was excited. Dad was matter of fact. He was a man who rarely showed his feelings, but I'm sure that somewhere deep inside there was a hint of a smile. Dad said he'd be at the airport with his newer Pontiac Laurentian station wagon to pick us up. Yes, by now his beloved '57 Ford Ranchero was a distant memory, resting in Ford heaven. The Pontiac had been a demo purchased from a Swan River dealer, a year-old bargain. Dad always looked for bargains.

By early evening, there we were at the terminal, strolling casually into the passenger waiting area. No security; no screening; no shoe removal, key removal, cash removal, or belt removal; no magic wands waving casually over private parts. There were just seats and windows and passengers, beyond which awaited a magnificent Boeing jet, waiting to take us as far as Thompson, where another aircraft would be waiting to whisk me and my dark-eyed bride on to Churchill.

At this point in my meander, I feel I must break a wee bit from Christmas 1970 to Christmas 1964. That was the last time I had flown to Churchill. I was a university student, short on holiday time because I had to sit around campus and write an exam on the twentieth. I simply did not have the time to spend two days on a train looking out the window at scenery I had seen before. Therefore, with financial help from my old man, I bought a ticket to fly home. I'd be there in hours, not days, and would return to Winnipeg by train after the holidays.

For the price of my ticket, I was to be treated to a well-used, and hopefully well-loved, DC-6. The plane was full and was to land in Thompson first to release many of the passengers and then go on to Churchill. Some of the passengers had been in Winnipeg shopping for Christmas, or others, like me, were simply going home for the holidays and the comfort of family.

Around eight o'clock on a cold, clear Saturday morning, the well-used, passenger-packed DC-6 departed Winnipeg and steadily and slowly climbed, passing over the Red River and the shores of the frozen Lake Winnipeg. It was like a moving atlas. I was captivated until, only about fifteen minutes after takeoff, one of the four engines began to belch black smoke. It dawned on me that this was one of those surreal moments when you realize you could be on the plane that made the national news that night. I could hear the headline read by a grim news anchor, "Plane plunges out of the sky onto a frozen lake. No survivors." The aircraft began a turn. The pilot announced we were returning due to technical difficulties, a fact that anyone with two eyes and a window to peer through could clearly see. It then began its slow descent back to Winnipeg. The lady sitting behind me was obviously terrified.

"Are we going to crash?" she asked frequently.

I had no answer, no reassurance, and really hoped not. I was, after all, a mere child of twenty-one, far too young to take the exit to Eternity Drive in a plane crash. As the aircraft banked and descended, a city patchwork of streets and houses loomed into view. Below, cars like Matchbox toys moved along snow-rimmed roads, and happy people, unaware of our predicament, ate breakfast and listened to "White Christmas" on the radio. I do clearly recall seeing a cacophony of urgent red flashing lights, probably gathered at the end of the runway just in case, and then hearing a thud as tires contacted concrete. We were safely down. The passengers, obviously relieved, cheered lustily because they realized they were not going to die after all, at least not on that day.

Ushered into the terminal, we became passengers without a plane to take us home, who loitered away the whole Saturday, nine hours of people watching, envying those who departed and arrived, while we sat. A complete waste of a day's holiday. Christmas music filled the air with the usual Christmas melodies. Rudolph still had a red nose, and the shoppers still hurried home with their Christmas gifts. The spirit of Christmas should have reminded me to be charitable, but that was difficult. And it became even more difficult as the sun sank around four o'clock. Two long hours later, my world now in total darkness, a public announcement declared that the delayed flight to Thompson and Churchill was now ready to board. And to the surprise of no one, the same old plane with a new crew awaited us. Thankfully, nine hours late, we took off and flew into the black void of a long northern night. Such was the adventure of northern flying in the 1960s. And, as an added bonus, all the thrills and excitement for the price of a ticket. A bargain indeed!

But 1964 was long gone. This was 1970, the dawning year in a shiny, new decade. And to compliment this shiny, new decade was a shiny, new jet, waiting to whisk us away. As flying was new for Val—she had flown just once before to Toronto and back—I was so glad to be in the comfort of a spanking-new Boeing jet and not in the well-used DC-6 of previous years. This flight to Thompson was everything my previous flight to Churchill had not been. It was incredibly quick. It seemed we were descending only a few minutes short of leaving behind the lights of Winnipeg.

Thompson's terminal was small and initially crowded. Most of the passengers claimed their bags and milled around and then departed as friends and family picked them up. A friendly agent urged the few remaining passengers still en route to Churchill. "Please sit. We'll have you on your way shortly." The plane, we were informed by an airline passenger agent, was being prepared. Thus notified, we attempted to make ourselves comfortable on very uncomfortable steel-and-plastic seats and awaited the call. As we waited, the wind outside began to stir, and each time the doors to the terminal opened, a flurry of snow blew in. Our fears began to grow that a threatening storm would prevent us from taking off. And to make matters more interesting, three or four Churchill-bound passengers had a bottle, which they were taking, secretly they thought, one at a time into the men's toilet. But few were fooled.

An hour after arriving in Thompson, the agent informed us our flight was ready. It was, indeed, a rollicking group that followed the agent, as could only be found in a northern community. Out into the drifting snow I went, like Good King Wenceslas, with Val following in my footsteps. In turn, I followed the post-Christmas revellers and the passenger agent who waved a flashlight around and told us to "please keep together" in a voice that was instantly snatched by the wind and carried into the darkened voids of the bush surrounding the airport. The field was snow driven and initially appeared empty until, looming into sight, there was a dimly seen outline that morphed into an ancient and, I suspect, battle-scarred veteran of World War II—a venerable DC-3. Weirdly, in the space of a few hours, we had time travelled, flying in a modern 1970s jet and then on to an ancient 1940s two-engine relic of history that, if truth be told, belonged in a museum.

Upon climbing some steps to enter the aircraft, we manoeuvred past our bags, which were tied down and stowed with straps. The aisle, which sloped up toward the cockpit, was of plywood and was kissed by a thin film of ice, and on each side, well-worn seats in pairs awaited us. The difficult part about reaching a seat was getting enough foot traction to climb the incline the floor presented. I recall thinking that the one consolation to this situation was that exiting would simply be an act of sliding, allowing gravity to do the work. Val later informed me that had we had the misfortune of being introduced to this aviation relic in Winnipeg, she would have turned around, demanded her money back, and gone home. That airline had done it again. Not only had it frightened the wits from me several years before on a Christmas flight home, but it was also now demanding a thief's ransom to fly in a museum piece, an aviation equivalent to the Model T.

The drunks who were on this flight claimed the very back seats and were making "zoom zoom" sounds and, birdlike, were flapping their arms and paddling their feet, as if riding a bike. At least they were having what seemed to be a good time, while we two were forced to hang on to seat backs to assist us in climbing the slippery slope and making our way toward empty seats near the front.

Thankfully, we sat down, Val next to a window so encrusted with frost that nothing could be seen, even if it had been daylight. She then reached for her seatbelt and—this is God's honest truth—one side of the seatbelt parted company with the seat. This necessitated a change to other seats and to a belt that, on the surface at least, appeared to work.

The doors of the DC-3 creaked closed. The windows were so thick with frost, and the plane so noisy and uncomfortable, that we could honestly not guess if it was airborne or if it wasn't. Val repeatedly tried to look out the frozen window as the aircraft moved almost as if it was in flight, but it wasn't. Then, the two engines roared even louder, and the stewardess announced above the noise that we were beginning liftoff. The venerable DC3 then struggled down the runway and droned steadily into the air, turning northeast towards our destination, Churchill. Our inebriated friends in the rear of the plane cheered, and the rest of the passengers broke into laughter and loud, raucous applause.

There was one stewardess on board, a pleasant young woman, wearing a heavy company parka and high winter boots. She offered us token refreshments: lukewarm coffee, crackers, and lumps of frozen cheese in individually wrapped packages. This was the fare provided for the fare demanded. This plus a flight on an obsolete museum piece. What a bargain!

To be honest, I cannot recall how long the flight to Churchill lasted. It was late, and I was cold, tired, even exhausted, as was Val, and we both dozed off, lulled by the steady drone of the engines.

With a start, I awoke. I had sensed that something was different. The plane was beginning to descend in wobbly lurches, and the steady drone of the engines changed note. Then, reassuringly, came the sound of grumbling hydraulics as the landing gear dropped and then locked into place. Suddenly, without warning, I felt a series of bumps as the wheels skimmed the runway and then I felt the reassuring jolt of frozen tires firmly on frozen concrete. At that moment, I knew I was home. We had arrived!

NEW YEAR, 1969–1970
THE LAST DANCE

True to his word, Dad was there, waiting patiently in the terminal. The flight was late, but he had learned that patience was required in the north. Time there plodded along, dictating its own pace, unlike the unseemly push and rush so characteristic of our big cities. Late arrivals, be they planes or trains, were taken as a matter of fact. Timetables were official statements only to be ignored with a "*C'est la vie,*" Gallic kind of shrug. Dad smiled and greeted me with an awkward man hug and greeted Val with a very English, very reserved kiss on the cheek. Although Val and I had been married for a year and four months, Dad barely knew her. After all, he rarely saw her; we lived a thousand kilometres apart. He was, to be truthful, a quiet man, and shy around strangers.

We retrieved our bags and departed the small terminal, out into a night that was devoid of even the hint of a breeze, out into the breathtaking cold of Churchill on a clear, quiet, late December night. It was quite the contrast to the snowy, blowy night we had left behind in Thompson. I do recall hearing the snow crunch hollowly beneath our feet with each step, and glancing up, I saw, as if for the first time, the star-rich spill of the Milky Way that, having lived in a light-drenched city in the south, I had long forgotten existed. That night in Churchill, the stars were breathtaking in their clarity, thousands of them, pinpoints of perfect light. Light that had started its race through space, moving at unimaginable speed on its journey toward the earth, and me. Light that originated in the depths of the universe, hundreds of light years away. Light that had set out on its travels long before Christ was born two thousand years ago. I recalled the words of a favourite carol, "Star of wonder, star of light, star with royal beauty bright," and realized that when it was written, most people on earth could look up and see the stars as a matter of course. This, regretfully, is not the case today.

Dad's car was parked nearby. By 1970, he had acquired a gently used 1966 Pontiac Laurentian station wagon. It was huge, quite the contrast to the 1957 Ford Ranchero he had previously owned. And being a Laurentian, it was basic. It had plastic-covered seats that froze solid in winter and were heat traps in the summer, hand-cranked windows, no radio, and a three-speed automatic transmission attached to a remarkably small six-cylinder engine. It was horribly underpowered and struggled on hills. But, if truth be told, this car was a huge step up, and it made the old man happy, which made Mum happy, which he knew resulted in a "happy wife, happy life."

Dad opened the tailgate, and I cast the bags into the cavernous hole behind the back seat. This car, when compared to our small 1969 Japanese Datsun, was General Motors huge. I could have parked our entire car in that Pontiac. Consequently, there was no problem with the three of us sliding onto the hard, cold, plastic-encased front bench seat: Dad behind the wheel, Val, by far the smallest of the three of us, in the centre, and I on the right. I closed the door, in anticipation of the short ride home. But instead of starting the car and backing out, as we expected, Dad just sat there. After a moment or two, I began to wonder if he had experienced a mini-stroke or some sort of paralyzing disorder. He said nothing but did have an annoying sort of half-knowing smile on his face, the kind of smile that said, "I know something you don't know." Val looked at me quizzically, motioning slightly with her eyes in the direction of the old man. I looked at her, shrugged, and then we both again looked at him. I began to wonder if Val's nursing skills would be needed, but more than likely they would not be, as she worked on the urology ward in the hospital. Then suddenly, with a rush of cold air, the rear passenger door opened, and a female voice trilled, "Hi George." Lo and behold, the very same pretty, leggy stewardess from our flight from Thompson who had served us warm coffee, crackers, and frozen cheese, while dressed in a company-issued mini skirt, top, and sturdy company parka, threw in a small overnight bag and slid in. Thoughts began to race in my head. Surely the old man, my dad, wasn't having an affair? After all, some of my friends' fathers had exchanged their older, well-used wives for newer, more streamlined models with fewer miles on the clock. But my old man? No way! He was, in my estimation, far too old and, quite honestly, this girl was ridiculously young and, I may add, very attractive. And to make my case absolutely beyond debate, no woman—no matter how pretty, how youthfully active, how generous in proportions—would replace my mother as the wife of my father. At least, I thought not and desperately hoped not. Dad then broke the ice.

"This is . . ." (I cannot recall her name, so let's pick one that was popular then and call her Carol).

"This is Carol," he announced.

Carol nodded and settled back onto the ice block that was the back seat. Then suddenly, she leaned forward and stuck out a hand in the direction of Valerie.

"Hi," she said.

She smiled and then, as if for emphasis, repeated her name.

"I'm Carol . . ." There was a pause. "And you are?"

She seemed to already know our names but asked anyway, a sort of introductory icebreaker.

Val introduced us, turning back as she talked.

"Hi Carol, I'm Val. And this is John."

I smiled, as if in pain, waved a hand, and grunted, "Hi."

Val also smiled. Carol nodded and returned the smile. Dad then took the opportunity of a pause in conversation to explain Carol's sudden appearance, a girl who, I must add, liked to talk. A lot. Silence seemed to bother her. She was driven by the urge to fill the air with the sound of her voice.

"Carol stays with Mum and me overnight between flights."

He had found a sufficient break in Carol's breathless chatter. Carol nodded in enthusiastic agreement and smiled again. Dad then explained that he and Mum had worked out a deal to board aircrew like Carol overnight. A sort of "you've got a girl; we'll take the girl" arrangement. Dad apparently picked them up, and Mum prepared the room and put together meals (although this girl, I suspected, would only need carrot and celery sticks).

As we drove home through the pitch dark of a long subarctic night, the car's headlights reflected off thousands of minuscule floating ice particles. And not another car was to be seen, just an empty road leading into the bitterly cold void. And Carol talked, mostly about herself. She was young, perhaps twenty or twenty-one, and had her life mapped out. Her future was bright and lay unhindered by roadblocks or diversions. Ah, the certainty of youth not yet scarred and battered by the reality of everyday life. And then, thank goodness, Dad pulled onto the snow-packed parking pad beside the back door of the house. Carol stopped her chatter, slid out of the back seat, and headed toward the house. We piled out, retrieving our bags from the car while Dad plugged in his car's block heater. And then we entered the warm yellow glow of the open kitchen door, where clouds of vapour layered out in swirls to meet the cold air. I was home. A place I had not been in over four years. And patiently, Mum waited for me and my new wife.

I was not too sure if Val would like Churchill. She was a big-city girl, born and bred. I was not a city guy. I had been small town for a lot of my life. She liked neighbours and neighbourhoods and nice lawns. I was indifferent to them. She liked the sounds and bustle of a city. I thought of myself as a small-town boy. I liked the peace and solitude that remote locations bring. She seemed to need the buzz of people nearby. We were and still are polar opposites, the perfect yin and yang, and like magnetic polar opposites, we attract each other.

With this in mind, we set off on the following day, a very overcast, dull late December day. I wanted to show Val my home, the place that shaped my formative years, so that she, by seeing what I had called home, could perhaps know me better. Mum lent Val her parka to replace the early-'70s fashionably short winter coat she wore in Winnipeg, and Dad generously lent me his Pontiac wagon, a rare event indeed. He trusted few with his car. So, taking advantage of this when-pigs-fly offer, off we went. I hoped to show Val as much as possible before the sun set by mid-afternoon. We had just over three hours.

From our house, we drove toward the mass of ancient grey rock, rock as old as the planet, rock that now forms a dark grey hem along the shores of Hudson Bay, sweeping as far as the eye can see, horizon to horizon, mile after mile, ice heaved and uneven, the tides still at work, super cold water still responding beneath the frozen surface to the gravitational pull of the moon. And sometimes, in the distance lay a dark streak of open water, even on the coldest of days. This was Val's first daylight "hello" to the place, her first peek.

And I was not too sure that she was initially impressed with the vast prairie-like emptiness of that vast frozen inland sea that lay before her. And as I drove on, deep within my bones, I sensed that Churchill was not exactly what I had remembered either. After all, I had not been home for four years, and time had slipped by all too easily. Time. One of the most precious gifts given to us that we tend to spend without thinking. And for me, school, work, and marriage had taken my time and my life in other directions. The old townsite was familiar but somehow felt different. Something felt missing. I felt the same winds blowing unimpeded off the bay. This was a given in Churchill, especially on short mid-winter days and long, cold winter nights. But the familiar came face-to-face with the reality that the winds were heralds of change, and not all change is necessarily good. Youthful energy and vitality had been the hallmarks of Churchill when I was young. But with the departure of the armed forces in the late '60s, much of the life had somehow been sucked out of the place. It seemed to be an elderly patient on life support. The buildings were still there in bricks and mortar and, like a shell on the beach, had once been home to life but now appeared empty. I sensed an impending loss. It was not what I remembered, and I was saddened. And, to knock the cherry off the cupcake, many of my friends were gone, scattered to the four winds, gone to create new lives elsewhere. I was reminded of the reality that change is the one constant in life and that change can be ruthless. Fort Churchill had passed her "best before" date, had aged, and was frail. At least, that is how I saw it. And I believe this is how Mum and Dad saw it. The unfortunate fact they faced was that this was the fate of any community with one major employer. With the departure of the armed forces, Churchill's *raison d'être* went with them, and the community went slowly into a financial tailspin.

As I drove Val around the almost-deserted roads that circled the base, roads that I had walked countless times, I was surprised to discover that my youthful world was so much smaller than I had recalled. There was the school and, across the road, the RCAF hangar and apron, strangely devoid of aircraft. There was the movie theatre, where I had worked evenings and spent many a Friday evening watching John Wayne swagger through nineteenth-century Texas or fight the Japanese on some Pacific Island in 1944. There was the hospital, where my sister, Eileen, was born. There was the arena, home of the blood feuds between the hated Navy team and anyone else. There were the curling rinks, where I had met Donna. There were the headquarters, the shared US and Canadian Army headquarters and the home of the only attempt for hundreds of kilometres at a patch of cultivated grass that was mowed. There was the launch site—where we students sought summer employment to pay for our education in the following year—which lay abandoned, as it had by then fulfilled its role. And there was the lonely wreck of the *Ithaca*, long since stripped of anything of value by locals. Then we were off down the highway; past Camp 20, the Inuit village; past the isolated and now empty HMCS Churchill, which in its prime time had been busy doing Lord knows what, as it was rumoured to snoop on the Soviets, and then on into the townsite, a place my friends and I were proud to call home. We called ourselves "townies"—as a badge of honour.

The town square was still there, a large gravel-surfaced space, still boasting its flagpole, two cannons, and a circle of white painted rocks. Atop the flagpole now smartly snapped the new Maple Leaf flag, the replacement for the old familiar Ensign. And to the west, over the highway in the direction of the flats and the Churchill River, was the CNR station, still very much an oddity whose architectural style was strangely out of place in this northern community. Built in the 1930s, it was a grand, fitting terminus to the Hudson Bay Railway and a place where, over the years, thousands of joyous hellos and tearful goodbyes had been said.

This was the station where, so many years ago, I had said my first hello to Churchill, with Dad waiting on the platform to greet Mum, me, and my brother as the giant black locomotive had snorted short jets of hissing steam into the cool, mid-'50s early morning August air. The memory of the walk down the puddle-strewn gravel road with our suitcases in tow, and the void, the inner emptiness I had felt at that very moment, still haunts me. For August, it had seemed cold, and the town that had lain before me had appeared colourless and on the very cusp of civilization. And there I had stood, friendless again. Little did I know then, but that town was to be my personal crucible, where the boy became a man, cast in the heat and fire of adolescence.

Pulling the car into the town square and parking close to the Hudson's Bay Company store, I followed Val, who made a determined foray into the premises to purchase small souvenirs for her family. Shopping, especially in department stores, has never been a favourite pastime of mine. Even today, after five decades of marriage, I feel uncomfortable wandering with the missus into the ladies' intimates department, with untouchable lacy whatnots hanging from racks, while Val chooses items and asks me, "What do you think?" when I truly have no opinion and feel the overwhelming urge to escape. My idea of shopping is to pick something—anything—and if it fits, purchase it, and run away as swiftly as possible. When I patronized The Bay in Churchill as a youth, it was usually to purchase only fishing lures, spools of fishing line, and boxes of .22 ammunition. Once the transaction was completed, I would leave. There really was nothing more to interest me in that store. And, I must add, my opinion has changed little over the last fifty years. The free-market economy would probably collapse if it depended upon me and my shopping whims.

With Val's shopping over, we continued on past the liquor store, a place where many memories, parties in the shack in Norm's backyard or down on the rocks, began. We would bribe someone who looked over twenty-one with the promise of a half bottle of rye, a bottle we called a "mickey," but I have no idea why, in exchange for the purchase of a twenty-six ouncer. We rarely failed, and not even once were we cheated by anybody who agreed to help us with our request.

With the liquor store behind us, we headed toward the National Harbours Board's property, passing the two tatty, tired-looking hotels in town: the Hudson Hotel and the Churchill Hotel. For reasons unknown, it was clear that originality in the naming of them was never, ever, a creative priority, and both were in desperate need of a new paint job.

It was the Churchill Hotel's vendor that was the source of most of the beer we consumed, purchased by bribing somebody. Again, finding somebody was never a real problem. The magic of the promise of free beer worked wonders. And, as a point of interest, it was to the Churchill Hotel that Wayne, Martin, and I headed on my twenty-first birthday to purchase my first legal case of beer. The date was May 25, 1964. We had to struggle through blowing snow to reach the vendor, where the clerk lectured me on not purchasing beer for any minor now that I was twenty-one, a warning which I gravely acknowledged with a nod. And, I must add here, the beer tasted much the same as it had before, I had reached the age of majority. The fact that I was then twenty-one removed the thrill of holding in my hand a cold bottle of Blue, the possession of which before my twenty-first birthday could have resulted in a local Mountie killjoy apprehending me and taking me home to the feigned wrath, but secret amusement, of the old man. He lived and survived by the creed, "Do whatever you want, just don't get caught." And, although I did not know this, the old man and the sergeant of the local RCMP detachment were Masonic Lodge brothers, and strings could be, and were on occasion, pulled.

The prominent downtown structure in Churchill is the Harbours Board's grain elevator, built facing the docks. At the time of its construction in the 1930s, it was reputed to be the world's second largest, with a capacity of two and a half million bushels. This building looms large over the town of Churchill and in the summer, hummed with activity, loading freighters, mostly with Saskatchewan-grown wheat bound for Europe. The port was exceptionally efficient, usually allowing a vessel to be docked, loaded, and then turned around to catch the tide within twenty-four hours.

The enormous shadow cast by the elevator was the product of the labour of countless concrete workers many years ago. One of those workers was Val's grandfather, Metro Melnyk, a Ukrainian immigrant who was, among many others, desperate for employment and laboured on that structure. I can only imagine how remote and alien Churchill must have been for him. And as for Val, just seeing that elevator was a link—a touchstone—connecting her to her family's history. What had, then, been just a story became reality, and she was moved. We took photos of the grain elevator that Val's grandfather or Gido, as he was referred to in Ukrainian, so that she could show the photos to her Mum, Sophie and Dad, John. Unbeknownst to Val, there was an earlier connection between Churchill and her mother's family of which we hadn't even been aware.

By mid-afternoon, the day had dwindled to a half-light that made more exploring difficult. I would have loved to have taken Val onto the rocks that rim the Bay, one of my favourite summer haunts, but it was out of the question. It was getting late. Besides, it was far too cold as it was winter, and a careless slip on the snow-covered surface might have led to a sprain or a broken limb or two. Therefore, I shelved that idea until a future summer visit, something that, to my regret, has yet to happen.

We spent the next six days at home with my parents, my six-year-old sister, the occasional stewardess, and a grumpy cat who had very definite ideas about which chair was his. Mum taught Val to knit, a skill that—fifty years later—she still practises, knitting sweaters and scarves and blankets for our grandkids, friends, and family. I get at least one new sweater a year. Dad, on the other hand, used his time well and watched television. TV had just recently arrived in Churchill in 1970, to supplement the CBC Northern Service radio station, CHFC. There was a local transmitter with the same power output as a toaster—which beamed previously recorded CBC television programs that were a week old. Thus, if it was Thursday, we watched the previous Thursday's programming, exactly one week later. It was like the movie *Groundhog Day* but in December. Because of the one-week delay, as New Year's Eve approached, the television subjected us to an increasing chorus of "Merry Christmas." And it was all in glorious black and white. You must understand that in 1970, there were no dishes on rooftops nor satellites streaming content "live and in living colour." No, nothing even remotely like that. Dad, however, was more than satisfied with this arrangement, even with the seven-day-old Saturday night hockey game.. Mum always said that Dad loved his television so much, he'd watch the test pattern if nothing else was available.

The evening of December 31 saw us invited to the New Year's Gala at the local Royal Canadian Legion Hall, our tickets a belated Christmas present from Mum and Dad. Dad was a veteran of the 8th Army who fought in North Africa, Sicily, and Italy, and he was always a staunch member of the legion. Val and I had a wonderful time with the crowd there, most of whom I had known for years and who were happy to meet my new wife. The funny thing was that I still introduced them as Mr. Smith or Mrs. Jones, despite the fact I knew their first names. Introducing them as Joe or Sally was unthinkable.

It was there, that evening, with Val and Mum drinking sparkly alcoholic beverages, and both giggling at secretly whispered topics, that I believe Val began to warm to the frigid North. There were cheesy nibblies, sausage bits on sticks, and—the pièce de résistance—Arctic char, all on a long foldaway table. There were also lots of laughs and hugs, and around eleven, as a farewell to 1970, there was entertainment by a few Inuit guests who spontaneously made the decision to "go out stepping" and perform a jig to welcome in the new year. The warmth of that evening stood in stark contrast to the realities of the community's grim economic uncertainty and the bitter subarctic chill outside, and the sad realization that Val and I would be leaving in less than forty-eight hours.

Two days later, we departed Churchill for the last time in the early days of January 1971. I was, like so many others, mostly young, leaving to face a lifetime of future unknowns, heading like the four winds to somewhere else. Some of us chose university and the professions, others, college, and the trades. Some worked in isolated bush camps or laboured on the dams. A few followed in family footsteps and joined the Forces or became police officers. Others, like the snows in spring, simply disappeared.

And this is why I am glad—so glad—that Val asked me what I wanted—really wanted—that long ago Christmas Eve of 1970. I am indebted to her for that question. If she had not asked, I would not have said, and we would have quietly stayed in Winnipeg and spent what would have probably been a New Year's Eve somewhere, with somebody, doing something quite forgettable. My Valerie gave me a gift that Christmas, the opportunity to say a final goodbye to a unique place. A special place.

Those six days marked the beginning of a new chapter, with a wife, sons on the horizon, and the building of lives together. And through the years, and then decades, that have slipped by, I can still clearly see the shadows of the past, floating like spectres in a dream. I see my friends—many gone—but then, young, and full of life. I see the noisy school classroom and the harried teacher. I see the crowded and equally noisy bus ride to and from school with that pretty Grade 10 temptress sitting comfortably on my lap. I see the shack in Norm's backyard, where we formed an appreciation for Canadian beer, fine Canadian spirits, and even finer cigars. I see the hormone-laden teen dances. I see the ancient rocks we climbed and challenged and sometimes fell from. I see our weekend expeditions into the bush. And I certainly see the girls—oh yes, the girls—who we had distant crushes on and with whom we stood absolutely no chance whatsoever. All this lives with me still, shadows that dance and swirl in that mysterious solitary space we call memory, shadows of a fortunate life well spent and well lived. A life of few, if any, regrets.

THE LOST CABIN IN THE WOODS: A POSTSCRIPT

The primal call of a small cabin, in the woods, near a lake, far from the madding crowd, is at the core of being Canadian. This call is a powerful part of our identity as a northern people who are confined within an enormous, lake-dotted landmass surrounded by three oceans and an immense border separating us politically, historically, and culturally from our quirky southern neighbours. This identity, being distinctly Canadian, begins with the rush of conception and then, piece by piece, is built into the web of our DNA as we grow and then emerge from the womb. From childhood onward, with the coming of summer, we yearn to leave behind the hurly-burly of the city, to be drawn irresistibly to the campfire and tent and sleeping bag, to experience the haunting call of the loon while canoeing on a silent, lonely lake. This is the Canadian experience, the Canadian dream.

The reality, however, is far different. For most of us, reality is bundling the kids, dog, and family cat into the SUV and then crawling down kilometres of highway, always apparently under construction and always filled with folks just like you, driving similar SUVs also stuffed with kids, dog, and the family cat. This migration ritual, come rain or shine, usually occurs on a summer Friday afternoon after work, with everybody heading in the same direction, to that place near a beach on a lake, to a place where you find the same neighbours you live near, work with, and play with in the city, all having simultaneously made the same decision to pull up stakes and move to the lake with you. Thus, the people you meet and nod to on walks, close to your cottage or campfire, are often the very same people you see shopping at home in the local supermarkets. The same kids, the same dogs, the same faces, the same middle-class values, but in a different location, a summer-place location. Anyway, that is the way I see it.

When I grew up in mid-twentieth-century Churchill, life was, to say the least, egalitarian. First, nobody I knew, none of my friends, enemies, nor their families, appeared to own their own homes and most certainly not a cottage. At that time, my parents found that existing in a rented home was challenging enough. Who would want to have the added aggravation of a second home, out of town, on a rocky, windswept Hudson Bay shoreline? A place which could quickly evolve into a perfect spot for polar bears to rendezvous, and we cottagers, on that windy, rocky stretch, could be just the right-sized snack polar bears were looking for to hold them over until the ice formed on the Bay. Cottages were simply out of the question, a privilege granted only to those middle-class southern city dwellers who liked to pretend they were roughing it in a cottage, unlike my mother, who certainly knew she was, beyond a doubt, roughing it in her rented Churchill townsite home. In a strange way, we lived in a cottage without realizing it. It fit, in most ways, the description of a basic cottage. We lived close to a beach, near a huge body of water; had no plumbing, flush toilets, nor running water; had uncertain electrical power; and were, as a community of dwellings, one of Manitoba's most isolated. Very cottage-like indeed.

As youngsters in our mid-teens, the group I hung with would, come late winter when the mercury would rise a little on the Fahrenheit scale, hike out into the woods. There, with our trusty single shot .22s, we would trudge along the Canadian National right of way or head out on the military Penguin Trail as it snaked its way south past Goose Creek. Sometimes as we walked the tracks, a train would approach, or on the trail, a conga line of sputtering army Penguins would appear, interrupting our travels and forcing us to move and stand on the verge, often in knee-deep snow, until the "all clear" occurred with the last of the noisy Penguins roaring by, casting track-hewn chunks of snow into the winter's air, or the last car of the train passed in a flurry of white. This escape into the bush, starting in March and continuing into spring, was a weekly event, held almost without fail every Saturday, weather permitting. By nine o'clock in the morning, we had made our jam and peanut butter sandwiches—which, by the way, we favoured because they stuck together in one piece—wrapped them, and jammed them into our parka pockets, along with a box of .22 shorts as well as long rifles, and a Zippo lighter or a pack of matches to light our cigarettes. As for water, a handful of snow served us well, shoved into our mouths to help wash down the peanut butter and jam sandwiches. And we would be gone until five or six in the evening, when, with the failing light, we returned down the tracks to home and, quite possibly, relieved parents glad to see we were safe and free of wounds from an errantly fired .22.

It was on one of these springtime expeditions we deviated from the security of the Penguin Trail and hiked deeper into the bush through even deeper snow. The woods were silent, save for our chatter, punctuated by the occasional pot shot of a .22 at a chasing shadow. It was on that hike, located in a clearing, we found, quite by chance, the cabin. It was constructed of logs and was perilously moving into a state of neglect. But it was, most certainly, a cabin in the woods, looking in the half-light of the light-filtered bush like a scene from a book of fairy tales. Someone approached and pushed at the door with the barrel of his .22. The door creaked open upon dry hinges. One small window barely illuminated the interior, which was one room with a dirt floor, a room in somewhat of a shamble, littered with a couple of broken chairs, with a table, homemade bunks along a wall, and a tin box stove. We didn't know who built it or when. Possibly, it could have been constructed years before, when the railway tracks were being laid in 1928. Maybe a trapper had built and later abandoned it. Or perhaps soldiers had constructed it as an exercise in survival skills. We had no idea. But of one thing we were certain. As far as we were concerned, it was a case of finders' keepers. And for the next three years, it became ours. Our home in the bush. And we cheekily claimed it. The creed we conveniently adhered to was that the cabin was ownerless, belonging to nobody at all. We were, it appeared, going to live the Canadian dream.

It was at this cabin, on Easter breaks, freed from the doldrums of school, we would spend the whole week, from Good Friday until the following weekend, happily away from our parents, feasting on food we had hauled in by sled. We all survived on stewed coffee made palatable with canned milk and spoonfuls of sugar, cans of baked beans, canned meats, and bacon and potatoes. No greens allowed.

And we were busy. I attempted to make a pair of homemade snowshoes from wood and wire. They worked, sort of, but were so heavy their purpose was self-defeating. They sank into the spring snow and got hopelessly tangled. We collected fresh snow in pots to have fresh water. And best of all, we explored the woods close to the Penguin Trail, something that was almost impossible to do in the summer because of the swarms of insects that filled the air. In the evening, we stoked the tin box stove, sat in the flickering light, smoked our hand-rolled cigarettes, and talked of girls named Mary Jane, Wanda, Julie, Barbara, Donna, or Carol—names you often heard then but don't hear much today, unless the girl in question is at least sixty-five or seventy.

Although we knew we had no legal title nor claim to the cabin, in our hearts, it was ours. We cared for it and, in our clumsy, youthful way, helped preserve it, helped it live on for perhaps a few years more. It served its purpose. It was our home away from home, our magical place in the woods.

Today, in the latter years of my seventh decade, sixty years later, all I have are memories and a few crinkled black-and-white photographs, showing the smiling faces of friends at the cabin, many of whom are now gone, passing on into what my good friend Wayne would laughingly call "The Great Perhaps." Thankfully, the gift of memory allows one to reside in a land where we are all still young and fearless, full of energy, with nimble limbs, and certain that life is an endless stream of tomorrows. And in that world of memories, we are flush with the vanity of youth. We still live, laugh, and defy all odds. The gods were then indeed kind to us, protected us. We were, after all, one of the immortals.

Is that cabin still there sixty years later? Perhaps. But the rational voice in my head says I have my doubts. But if by chance it is, then I hope other youngsters have also, quite by accident, stumbled upon it just as we did in that fairy-tale way and have laid temporary claim to it. And, come to think of it, don't we all—every one of us, in one way or another—have our own secret cabin to discover lying deep in the woods? A cabin that, when it is time, we pass on to others? After all, is this not how life should be? I certainly hope so.

The End

ACKNOWLEDGEMENTS

I would like to acknowledge those who made this trip with me into a world long passed. Without them, this would be a blank page. And if I do miss somebody, chalk it up to my being well into my seventies, an excuse I find, on occasion, most useful. I am old enough to use age as an explanation for forgetting to pick up milk or bread, or even for forgetting the occasional birthday, but I am still sharp enough, despite my age, to retain my driver's licence. A most happy balance, and long may it continue.

And now to my list of those who, in one way or another, helped shape my life. Mostly first names only. To my one and only for over half a century partner, Val. You are my North Star. I'd be lost without you.

Thank you to George and Rose, my parents who made the difficult decision to leave their home in England and move to a new land. To my brother Ivan, who kept in touch with us in Churchill even while serving at sea, and to Ivan's wife, Lin, always a support. To my brother Geoff, who was there with me, and to my sister Eileen, a late arrival in life and the first of our family born in Canada.

Thank you to my sons Ian and Graeme for their help and unwavering support during the writing of this book. To my busy daughters-in-law, Lainie and Louisa, for their encouragement. And to my lovely granddaughters, Hollie, Lacey, and Isla, who were the inspiration for writing this book. I want them to know their roots. Big thanks to my niece and nephew, Kristen, and Mike. I couldn't have finished this without you. At my age, I tend to wander, and you put me back on track.

Thanks to Ronnie; Norm; Wayne and Linda Langlois, Wayne's parents, Mr. and Mrs. L; Mr. O, Norm and Sharon's dad; Freddie; Wayne S; Doug;

JoAnne; Artie; David; Bill A and his sister Dianne; Jack and Gloria Jean; Susie; Mr. C and the beautiful Mrs. C; Scottie; Larry; the girls who rode the school bus with us; Hector the scholar; Eddie, the classic New Yorker and American Army brat; Johnny P; the Wilson sisters; and whomever else I may have forgotten.

To those of you still with us, I do remember you and wish you well. And to those who have scooted off the highway of life down some exit, an exit heading to what my friend Wayne laughingly called "The Great Perhaps," may you forever be sunning yourselves, ordering a cocktail or two while lying on recliners by the pool. I'll be seeing you. But not too soon, I hope.

Printed in Canada